MOM
ENTREPRENEUR
Extraordinaire

Top experts share strategies for success

In collaboration with the Direct Selling Women's Alliance

Sharon,
To your
extraordinary
success!
Audrey
Godl
4 28 12

THRIVE
PUBLISHING™

THRIVE Publishing
A Division of PowerDynamics Publishing, Inc.
San Francisco, California
www.thrivebooks.com

ISBN: 978-0-9829419-2-8

Library of Congress Control Number: 2010942217

Printed in the United States of America on acid-free paper.

We dedicate this book to you,

the mother and business owner, who recognizes the importance of having your inner and outer life working together in a way that brings clarity and peace of mind to you, and to those you love. We salute you for embracing your powerful role in life—and we celebrate your commitment to being the best you can be!

The Co-Authors of *Mom Entrepreneur Extraordinaire*

Table of Contents

Acknowledgements

Gratitude is an essential element in every good life, and no one knows it better than a mom entrepreneur.

Before we share our wisdom and experience with you, we have a few people to thank for turning our vision for this book into a reality.

This book is the wonderful concept of Caterina Rando, the founder of THRIVE Publishing™ and a respected business strategist, with whom many of us have worked to grow our businesses. Working closely with many extraordinary mom entrepreneurs, Caterina realized how valuable the dual role of mother and business owner is in today's society, how most mom entrepreneurs can learn from the know-how and ingenuity of other mom entrepreneurs, and how to make it all work.

Without Caterina's "take action" spirit, her positive attitude and her commitment to excellence, you would not be reading this innovative book, of which we are all so proud.

Additionally, all of our efforts were supported by a truly dedicated team who worked diligently to put together the best possible book for you. We are truly grateful for everyone's stellar contribution.

To Ruth Schwartz, with her many years of experience and wisdom, who served as an ongoing guide throughout the project, your leadership and support of our production team are deeply appreciated.

To Erin Sarika Delaney, whose care in working with the co-authors and copyediting their work proved highly valuable and ensured that this book would be the best it could be.

To Tammy Tribble, who brought her creative talent and brilliance to the design of the book, thank you for your enthusiasm, problem solving and exquisite attention to what looks good.

To Bernie Burson, Karen Gargiulo, Hester Lox and Rua Necaise, who provided us with keen proofreading eyes, thank you for your support and ongoing contribution.

We also acknowledge each other for delivering outstanding insights, heartfelt guidance and sincere advice. Through our work on this book and our work in the world and at home, we are deeply committed to enhancing the lives of others, inside and outside our homes. We are profoundly grateful that we get to do work that we love and make a contribution to so many in the process. We do not take our good fortune lightly. We are clear in our mission—to make a genuine contribution to you, the reader. Thank you for granting us this extraordinary opportunity. We are grateful for your trust.

The Co-Authors of *Mom Entrepreneur Extraordinaire*

Introduction

Congratulations! You have opened an incredible resource, packed with great ideas that will enhance your life in ways you cannot yet imagine. You are about to discover the magic that creates a mom entrepreneur extraordinaire.

The success of your personal and professional life comes as a result of more than just talent, commitment and hard work. Your success is determined by your own self-awareness, the systems and plans you create to support you and the way in which you honor the things that matter most to you. We know you want to be the absolute best you can be as a mom and as an entrepreneur.

With this book, you will quickly learn from other successful mom entrepreneurs who will assist you in juggling your responsibilities for both work and family. As top experts in each of our respective specialties, we've joined together to give you powerful tools to support your optimal success and capabilities, as both an entrepreneur and a mom. Each of us has seen how even small changes in our actions, attitude and behavior can transform and uplift our lives and our businesses.

All the mom entrepreneurs you will meet in this book want you to live your life with ease and fulfillment. We have outlined for you our top tips and included the most expert advice we have to enhance your business and family life, from how to master business travel with your children to how to build your profession through blogging, branding and networking; from how to achieve your goals through persistence and savvy to how to create time just for you.

To get the most out of *Mom Entrepreneur Extraordinaire*, we recommend that you read through this book once, cover to cover. Then go back and follow the advice that applies to you, in the chapters most relevant to your current situation.

Every improvement you make will make a difference in how you feel about yourself and how you perform your work at home and when you are out in the world. It will also make an enormous difference in the lives of those around you.

Know that just learning what to do will not transform your career or your family life. You must take action and apply the strategies, tips and tactics we share in these pages. With our knowledge and your action, we are confident that you too will master the world of being a *Mom Entrepreneur Extraordinaire* and reap the many wondrous benefits it offers.

To your unlimited success!

The Co-Authors of *Mom Entrepreneur Extraordinaire*

You Can Have It All

Running a Business Your Family Will Love

By Molly Klipp

You are walking out the door to go to work, kids are crying, one of them is hanging onto your skirt. The dog is barking. The garbage is overflowing. The kitchen is a mess and your husband is asking when you are coming home. Sound familiar?

Being an entrepreneur takes a special mindset. It takes being able to see the bigger picture, the long-term goal and the snapshot of what you want for you and your family. It requires you putting yourself and your family inside a bubble of positive energy with a dream of the way you want your life to look. As an entrepreneur with a family, you need to realize that you are not operating on an island. Your family plays a huge part in your success and the success is so much sweeter when everyone works together to build the dream.

Do you give your family a reason to be part of your business? What part of your business can you involve your husband and kids in? What decisions could they be a part of? Do they know what you are working for? Make them a part of your dreams and goals. Never get so absorbed in your own visions and aspirations that you cut your loved ones off or make them feel left out. That said, where do you begin?

Hot Tip #1: Begin With Your Spouse

Good for you if you are a single mom entrepreneur. Otherwise, if you are married or have a significant other, this is where you begin. This is the person you sit down with and make a plan of what you want your life to look like. When you have a family, it is not all about you. Your number one person, your partner in life, is vital to making this all work. If you are single, the same questions below apply. You may want to find a supportive friend or family member to go over these questions with you. Be specific. Be detailed. Make a list.

- Do you want your home to be the "perfect" home?

- Do you want your home to be the place where all the kids come to play?

- Do you want a quiet home?

- Do you have a nanny or want one?

- Do you want controlled chaos in your home?

- Do you want a large yard to care for or have someone else care for?

- Do you want a pool, lake or sports court?

- Do you want to entertain? Adults or children, or both?

- Do you want a home that is already completed or something that is a work in progress?

- Do you have time to do the work in progress?

- Where do you want your children to go to school?

- Are vacations as a family important?

- As an entrepreneur, are you working inside the home or outside the home?

- How many children do you want to have and do you plan on having any while building your business?

Your home is your family's life center and holds the answers to the above questions or other questions of your own. These answers are vital to how everything else in your life flows.

Hot Tip #2: Involve Your Children

No matter what the ages of your children, you can involve them in your business. It can be as simple as the baby being held by Dad, a sibling or a nanny as you drive away waving and they yell to you, "Knock 'em dead, Mom!" When my children were little they got confused and yelled, "Beat 'em dead, Mom!" Oh, the joys of motherhood! That habit has stayed throughout my career and my children and husband always wish me luck as I head out the door to a home show, training or speaking engagement. Knowing your family is behind you is a great motivator.

As your children get older, find jobs they can do to help you in your business. I don't mean emptying the dishwasher! Find jobs that directly relate to your business. For example:

1. Folding mailers and stuffing envelopes

2. Loading or unloading your car with your briefcase, samples, products and so on

3. Updating your email list

4. Answering the phone, taking messages and orders

5. Packing boxes with products

6. Being the maid or butler for company parties at your home and helping you prepare for meetings outside your home

7. When they get smarter than you on the computer, have them do your email flyers and your website

These are just a few possibilities. As we all have different businesses, the jobs will vary. For more ways your kids can contribute, see Grace Keohohou's chapter on *Creating a Family Home-Based Business* on page 13.

Pay them for the jobs they do for you and thank them for jobs well done. This makes them feel a part of what you are building and makes them feel like an official part of the team.

Hot Tip #3: Hire a Housekeeper and Perhaps a Nanny

Hire a housekeeper, even if you can only have someone in once a month. It is a total stress reliever and reward for your hard work. There is something wrong with having to work all day or evening and then coming home and having to clean the toilets.

If you have young children not yet attending school, get a nanny, live-in or live-out—you choose what works best for you. I have two sets of children who are twelve years apart. When I started in Aloette Cosmetics® in 1982, my oldest daughter Kerry was two years old and Keegan was eight months old. I cared for them, the house and my business by myself. However, at the time I had a much smaller house, and my business was just beginning.

When my second set of children, Maggie and Rudy, came in the early '90s, we had our Seattle franchise with an office staff and a growing business. With two children in school and two at home, a nanny became a necessity for us, as well as a blessing. If you can, hire a nanny who will cook, clean and take care of your kids. Your stress level will decrease quickly.

Hot Tip #4: Have Family Meetings

Hold family meetings every month, discussing what the goal is for your business and how everyone can help. Important suggestion: have a meeting with your spouse *before* the family meeting to discuss what the topics will be. Prepare the agenda together.

Hot Tip #5: Include the Kids in Your Sales Efforts

Set a sales quota or goal for the next month for your business and discuss it at the meeting. Let the children know that when they help out by cooperating, doing their chores, making your life simpler and encouraging you, that you will gift them with something they want.

A suggestion that worked great for us was to find out what each of the kids wanted, like new shoes, a toy, movie tickets or new jeans. When they helped me out and we hit our goal, they received what they requested. It was a win-win!

Make a jar for each child, and have them write slips for the different items they want as rewards. Give them a price limit that works for you. Choose something out of the jar for each child when they have helped you hit a goal for your business.

Hot Tip #6: Plan Your Calendars Together

During your monthly family meetings, have everyone pull out their individual schedules and calendars. If you have younger children who do not have calendars, yet *you* know their schedule—their soccer games, volleyball, ballet, birthday parties, class events and so on—put those in your monthly calendar so that you have a master calendar of your family's life in one place. You may or may not be able to attend all of the events, and you will know where everyone is at all times and where they are supposed to be. Different colored pens for each family member is also helpful. Remember Dad, too!

It may seem easier to have a family calendar and a separate business calendar. However, you don't want to get caught scheduling a business appointment and forget that your daughter had a volleyball game you promised to attend. We try so hard to be organized, and when we don't prioritize our family before our business appointments, the family suffers. For more detailed information on managing your time and many priorities, see Martha Staley's chapter on *The Art of Leveraging Your Time* on page 113.

Hot Tip #7: Keep Your Family a Priority

In the early years of my business my husband said to me, "You are nicer to your consultants than you are to your family and we will be around a lot longer." That hit me right in the heart and I never forgot it.

One of the main reasons most of us became entrepreneurs was to give us the ability to work our own schedules, be our own bosses, earn the money we deserve and be available to our families. However, because we love what we do, we can get consumed working on our business and wind up excluding the ones we love. Find ways to make your family a priority in your life. Here are some suggestions:

• **Have dates with your spouse.** Schedule a date night with your partner at least once a month. Get season passes to plays, games or something else that requires you to meet at a scheduled time. Take time to talk to each other about your dreams and goals— not just about business or the kids. Unless you schedule this, you will find excuses why you can't take the time. Remember to always treat each other like you are dating and think of the other person first. Surprise each other with special dates. Enjoy your special time together.

- **Have dates with your children.** Talk to your children, find out how they feel about your business, what makes them feel important and what makes them feel unimportant. Have "date nights" with your kids individually and really listen to what they have to say. They will tend to talk to you more about other things as well.

- **Plan vacations together.** Write a list of places you would like to go. Have the kids research different vacation spots online and don't set any price limitations. You might be surprised with what they choose. You can then plan a family vacation and involve them in the process of hitting the goal you have for your business so you can go on the vacation they chose. Plan both extended vacations and weekend vacations. A weekend away in the middle of winter at a local hotel with a pool can be a big event to an eight-year-old.

If you were to ask my kids what their favorite memories of my being an entrepreneur was, they would say the trips. My kids have traveled the world on business trips and the best ones were when we mixed them with family time. You can go first for the business trip and then have them join you after your business is finished so you can have alone time with your family. Or perhaps you can take them on a trip you earned with your business. For more information on traveling with children, see Cindy Sakai's chapter, *From Business Suit to Bathing Suit*, on page 125.

Hot Tip #8: Be the Example

This is perhaps the most important tip I can give you. My mom used to tell me that the mother is the heartbeat of the home. Everything revolves around what Mom does and thinks, and how she acts. As mothers, we carry a heavy responsibility to be the prime example of how we want our children to behave. Do we want our children to respond rationally or react irrationally?

Encarta Dictionary says the definition of *respond* is: "to say or write something in reply." The definition of *react* is: "to act or do something in reaction to something else." Have you ever seen one of your kids react in a way that surprised you and then realized later that they have duplicated one of your reactions? Scary, isn't it?

I believe that God has given us the responsibility as parents to teach *response* instead of *reaction*. As entrepreneurs, we are teaching our children valuable life lessons in business, as well as in living and life relationships. How we behave daily sets the standard for how our children develop as adults. My mission is to show my kids through my example how to work through challenges, how to celebrate successes and how to deal positively with failures.

Through the 28 years that I have been an entrepreneur, the most important lessons were those that I was able to pass on to my children. Did they learn everything I wanted them to? Probably not, yet when I talked with each of them, three of them being adults now, I was surprised and honored at what they had to say.

My 30-year-old daughter Kerry said, "Seeing my mom have the strength and courage to take on her own business and anything that came along with it, while making sure to be at every event of my youth, showed me that everything is possible in life. Settling for less is not an option."

Keegan, my 29-year-old, stated, "Whenever my mom said that she was going to accomplish something, she did because she would figure out a way to make it happen. I watched her evolve, learn and develop to become the mom and the entrepreneur she is today."

Realize that your children watch you and learn from you and that your daily actions actually empower them every day to be the best they can be in every avenue of their lives. Your kids may be younger and working for better grades, or to be the lead of their high school play, or adults working to achieve their own goals; your daily disciplines show your kids how daily habits really do matter. Whether they become an entrepreneur themselves or a star employee with an entrepreneurial spirit, they will be far happier and more successful in their adult life having learned from one of the best people possible—their mom.

Having your own business as a mom entrepreneur is not just about making more money, or even having your own schedule. Sometimes it is just having the ability to use your creativity, and becoming the person you always wanted to be. That creativity trickles down to your children and allows them to express themselves in their own individual ways.

Maggie, my 18-year-old daughter, puts it like this: "My mom's leadership skills and determination have helped me develop into a leader as a captain on my sports teams and with leading parts in drama productions."

In the end, the most important people in your life are your family members, and sometimes just "being there" is more important than anything. I was blessed with a business that allowed me to have my office in my home. My youngest son, Rudy, age 17, put it like this: "What I love is that it's not like most kids' parents where they have to wait until the end of the day to see them. I get to come home from school and give my mom a hug and a kiss because she is always there."

Isn't that the reason most of us moms became entrepreneurs— finding a way to balance our family and our career successfully?

Spread Your Wings and Grow

What opportunities have been offered to you that could change your and your family's lives forever? I challenge you to spread your wings. Pick something you love. Have a family meeting, plan a trip, get those jars out, find out what you and your children want to work toward, and plan date nights. Above all, take the risks, put in the effort, have fun and don't look back. Be true to yourself and be the best you can be. You never know whose lives you will touch. Maybe it will be the lives of the most important people in your life—your family.

Molly Klipp

President
Aloette Cosmetics of Seattle
You Can Have It All
(425) 742-7651
molly@mollyklipp.com
www.mollyklipp.com
www.aloetteofseattle.com

Married since 1977, the mother of four wonderful children and one beautiful grandson, Molly has always known her priority in life is her family. Becoming an entrepreneur while her two oldest were babies started Molly's journey in balancing her family and her career. Molly has been in sales leadership since 1982 and she has mentored and coached thousands of individuals to greater heights. In 1985 she started Aloette Cosmetics of Seattle, and has sold over $25 million in product with her dynamic sales team.

Molly is an image consultant and co-author of *Image Power*, published by PowerDynamics Publishing in 2008. Her specialty is providing expert makeovers using color, accessorizing, wardrobe planning and makeup tips for corporate groups that are looking to improve their professional image. She coaches, holds teleseminars, and speaks to moms looking to balance their business with ease.

Whether speaking on sales, image, or balancing family and business, Molly's fun and energetic speaking inspires women to take it to the next level. Molly has joyfully experienced life as a stay-at-home mom, dynamic business leader, professional trainer and speaker, as well as a student pilot—all while keeping her family as the center of her life. She believes in being an example for her children so they can be the people they choose to be.

Creating a Family Home-Based Business

Working in Harmony for Greater Success

By Grace Keohohou

"People who have good relationships at home are more effective in the marketplace."
—Zig Ziglar, American speaker and author

There are many people who desire a home-based business and yet do not feel certain about how to engage their loved ones in the idea. Often in traditional business, family life and career are separated. The family is rarely involved in or aware of the trials and wins that take place in the office on a day-to-day basis. As a mom entrepreneur, you commonly work from home, which automatically connects your family life and business. What a blessing!

To create the best possible connection requires a shift in focus from "my business" to "our family business," creating a sense of collaboration. This makes the journey more fun, profitable and rewarding.

Blessings of Being a Mom Entrepreneur

I was raised by parents who were both entrepreneurs, and I learned some of the ins and outs of that lifestyle early on. It was a fascinating life and one that I am grateful for.

Here are some of the benefits:

- I heard how my parents communicated with people over the phone, and I learned how to talk to others with respect and great enthusiasm.

- I was able to be a part of their excitement for the adventure and learned how it was not about the destination—it was about the journey.

- I had the opportunity to be involved in the business and felt I played an important role starting at a young age.

Even though I did not necessarily appreciate my mom being a mom entrepreneur all the time, I certainly applied much of what I learned from her to my own life. I know that my children and your children will do the same. They are constantly watching, observing and embracing things we do, consciously or unconsciously. By watching you, they can be inspired to embrace their own life with passion, commitment, dedication and motivation.

The entrepreneurial world teaches things that the traditional business schools do not teach. When I was young we would take rides in the car, and instead of listening to music, we would listen to motivational programs. Back then, of course, I was not so enthusiastic about that. In fact, I would beg my mom to play something different—anything! Eventually I noticed how the words I listened to made a difference in how I lived my life. Now, years later, my own daughter asks if she can listen to my iPod®. I tell her she can, and that it is filled with motivational talks. She often chooses to listen anyway. I know it is benefiting her as it did me.

My parents used to talk about enlightened vocabulary. They taught me how to reframe any negative thought or phrase into a positive one. They taught me to communicate in a way that inspires me and those with whom I surround myself. For example, there was a time when I would say to my children, "Mommy is working very hard." When I became aware of my words and what effect they were having, I chose to shift that language to, "I am working smart today. I'm creating ways to be more effective." I wanted them to know the joys of doing something they are passionate about, and that it does not necessarily require hard work—smart work creates an abundant life as well.

Being a mom and entrepreneur is not always easy. There were certainly times of trials and tribulation in my own parents' entrepreneurial life. However, they always shared with us what was happening and they did so in a positive, honest and lighthearted way. They let us know when they were making major shifts that affected us, and they were always careful about how they presented it to us. For example, when we had to change from having whatever we wanted to having to be on a tight budget, my parents said, "We are wisely budgeting our money and investing properly. We are making beneficial adjustments in our lifestyle right now."

From this, I learned that every stage of life is good and holds great value. Though our budget adjusted, our connection as a family and care for each other did not change. We were in it together as a team. I learned how to appreciate money, invest wisely, and find the benefit and opportunity in any circumstance.

Now as a mom and entrepreneur, when my own children ask for something I say, "Is this something that you really want or is it something that you need?" There is a difference. We always have the opportunity and the responsibility to make wise choices that will benefit all. How are we going to best use our resources? How are we going to enjoy what we created? How are we going to celebrate our success? How are we going to share and contribute what we have to make a positive difference?

Steps to Creating a Family Business

First, clarify what is driving you to build a home-based business. Here are some specific questions you can ask yourself to get clear:

• What makes this business important to me?

• How will this business benefit my family and me?

• What will it take for my family to embrace our business?

• What am I willing to do to ensure this business is a success?

• How will I feel when we make the vision for our business a reality?

Second, request a family meeting to open the lines of communication and discuss the business. This will give you an opportunity to invite them to play an active role in creating a home-based business that is rewarding and enjoyable for everyone. The following are some key questions to ask your family members during the meeting:

• What do you think about making this a family business rather than just Mom's business?

• What do you feel are your greatest talents?

- How do you see yourself participating or contributing to the success of our business?

- How would you like to benefit as a family?

- How would you like to be rewarded personally?

- When would you like to begin?

- What are our next steps?

This initial family meeting will serve as a healthy starting point or new beginning and engage the family in the journey. Be sure to celebrate the fact that it is a step forward to creating something special for all who participate. By creating a family business you build a bridge rather than a barrier between your loved ones and your career.

Bridges Versus Barriers

As a result of years of research and connecting with home-based entrepreneurs from all walks of life, I have found that creating harmony with work and family can be a major challenge area. A lot of people are carrying a tremendous amount of guilt. They feel guilty when they are investing time in their business and should be present with their family, or they feel guilty when they are sharing time with their family and giving less time to their business. This cycle of guilt is an emotional drain that serves no one. There is light at the end of the tunnel. Here are a few suggestions to help overcome the guilt and build bridges at the same time.

1. Be present. When you are with your family, give them your full focus and attention. A wise person once shared with me that our children often measure love with time. The more quality time we share with them, the more loved they feel. Notice I said *quality* time.

It is not the amount of time that counts—it really is the quality of time that is measured.

When you are investing time in your business, give it your full attention as well. I use a timer that helps me stay focused on my priorities and the action items that will give me the greatest return for my time investment. If you are clear about the emotional reasons that are driving you to build your business in the first place, every move you make will be intentional. Be present right where you are.

"It's not what if, it's what now."
—Author Unknown

2. Set a schedule. Prepare a family calendar that is available and visible to the entire family. Each family member is expected to provide you with his or her school and extracurricular activities, special events and important days for each month. Give each person a timeline to submit that information to ensure it is included as a priority. This will allow you to coordinate your family schedule with your business schedule. Remember, you won't be able to make every choral performance or volleyball game. One thought is to provide each person with two star stickers every month. Those are to be placed by their "must attend" events, the ones at which they would really like you to be present. If you are able to go to some of the other scheduled activities it is a bonus, not an expectation.

Include in the calendar your business meetings or home shows. This way your family knows that your activities are as important as theirs.

3. Follow through. When you under-promise and over-deliver, it is remembered. When you over-promise and under-deliver, it is remembered. A great rule of thumb is to assess what you are truly capable of delivering within the time frame requested. It is important to have a daily calendar or accomplishment list that will help guide your activities throughout the day, week and month. This will set you up for success in many ways. At a glance you will be able to see how little or how much more you can squeeze into your schedule and still ensure follow-through.

There are several options for tracking daily activities. One example is to create a top ten list each day. List the top ten activities that you choose to accomplish for a given day.

Another strategy is one that I learned in a teleclass. Begin by dividing a piece of paper into four equal parts and label in the following way: Urgent—Important, Important—Not Urgent, Urgent—Not Important and Not Important—Not Urgent. Then begin to fill in the boxes accordingly. Here is an example of what that may look like for you:

Box 1: Urgent—Important	Box 2: Important—Not Urgent
1. Contact team leaders to assist with Monday night meeting 2. Pick up Isea's football gear for this week's game	1. Call ten leads to book career conversations 2. Make doctor's appointment for tests
Box 3: Urgent—Not Important	**Box 4: Not Important—Not Urgent**
1. Read new shipping policy 2. Drop off dry cleaning	1. File paperwork on desk 2. Look for new vacuum

This is a great way to divide your daily business and family tasks to ensure you are maximizing each moment.

"It was character that got us out of bed, commitment that moved us into action and discipline that enabled us to follow through."
—Zig Ziglar, American speaker and author

Ways to Contribute

There are a variety of ways each person can contribute to the success of the business. Again, refer back to the original family meeting. What talents did each person say they had, how did they feel they could best contribute, and what were they willing to do? Their ideas are great starting points. Be sure to find tasks that make the most sense for their age and talents and set them up to feel like they are making a positive difference. The following are some additional possibilities:

- Filing paperwork

- Entering orders

- Labeling product or marketing materials

- Packing and unpacking promotional materials and products

- Stamping letters

- Stuffing envelopes

- Entering business cards into your contact database

- Writing thank you notes

- Wrapping gifts for clients or colleagues

- Emptying garbage

- Labeling files

- Filling the printer with paper

- Taking an inventory of supplies

- Refilling supplies

- Making a shopping list

- Filling out deposit slips

- Opening, paying and filing bills

- Shredding documents

- Cleaning, vacuuming and dusting the office

- Checking voicemails and documenting them

- Making follow-up calls

- Scheduling appointments

- Organizing the family calendar of events

- Making copies

- Collating paperwork

- Assisting with household chores

Again, think of things that don't necessarily require your greatest talents and skills. When you discover ways to delegate projects and stay focused on the activities that provide you the greatest return on your investment of time, your business and quality time with family will grow profoundly.

> *"If you would thoroughly know anything, teach it to others."*
> —Tryon Edwards, American theologian

Expect Success

There are many reasons I am personally grateful to have been raised in an entrepreneurial environment my entire life. The philosophies of a family business provided a variety of benefits that most children do not have the pleasure of experiencing. I must share that it was not always easy, yet I would not change a thing about it. The skills and lessons taught accelerated my success, and for that I am grateful beyond measure.

Here are some suggestions for a successful life as a mom and an entrepreneur:

• Have a servant's heart.

• Focus on enriching and empowering the world.

• Have a possibility mindset, an eagerness to learn and grow.

• Make goal-setting a regular practice.

• Look for ways to make dreams real.

• Have a powerful work ethic and dedication.

• Have the capacity to be a courageous risk-taker.

• Develop the power of mind management.

• Have an understanding of careful word selection.

• Be passionate about life and people.

• Have methods to support maintaining a positive attitude.

• Have the awareness that each person can make a difference.

- Know that actions can influence generations.

- Embrace the pleasure of truly living on purpose.

Being a mom entrepreneur is one of the greatest gifts we can give to our children and future generations. I am grateful every day that I get to say that I work from home, that I am a mom and an entrepreneur, and that I get to involve my children in that process. It is a blessing to raise my children in this powerful mindset and way of life.

By being a mom entrepreneur, you are indeed a living model for your children and they will become your reflection. Be the best model you can be. Show them the joy of your work and do not be afraid to show them the not-so-easy times as well. Show them that your love for them never changes. Invite them to make wise, healthy choices in their own words and actions. Engage them in philanthropic efforts. Invite them to live the life that they want to live while you are living the life of your dreams.

Grace Keohohou

President and Co-Founder
Direct Selling Women's Alliance

(888) 417-0743
grace@dswa.org
www.dswa.org
www.gracefulspeaking.com

Grace Keohohou co-founded the Direct Selling Women's Alliance with her business partner and mother, Nicki Keohohou. The DSWA is an association that serves organizations and individuals through a resource-rich website, leading-edge training, and strategies relevant to growing a direct selling business.

Today, Grace is reaching entrepreneurs in more than 30 countries through her speaking, writing and educational programs. She is a co-author of the best-selling books, *Build it Big* and *More Build it Big* published by Kaplan Publishing, and she also collaborated on a children's book series called *The True Princess*, created to build self-esteem in children.

Grace is a certified coach with the Coach Excellence School, credentialed by the Worldwide Association of Business Coaches (WABC). She was recently named the National Advocate of the Year for Working Mothers and the 4th Most Influential Woman in the International Direct Selling Profession.

Grace partnered with her children to create a grassroots program called Kids4Kids, based in Hawaii. The program was created to help raise money and school supplies for children in need. Kids4Kids partnered with OfficeMax® and together they are making a difference.

Growing Your Business While Growing Your Family

By Sarah Kalicki-Nakamura, MAOM, CDC

I am an accidental entrepreneur. I never thought about opening my own business. However, I have now owned TH!NK, LLC, for more than a decade, and I owe this wonderful experience to motherhood, thus making me a mom entrepreneur.

Let me take you back in time so that you can better understand my story and the foundation of the tips I'm giving you in this chapter. Twelve years ago, I was a career woman working in Hawaii with a crystal clear plan of how to climb the corporate ladder in the hospitality industry. I was married to a wonderful man—I still am—and we had a great weekend lifestyle of hiking, mountain biking, camping and swimming. I was not in the mindset of having children.

As I have since learned, there are my plans and there are God's plans. In 1998, I found out that I was pregnant. I did not jump up and down for joy. In fact, I sobbed for hours as I realized that life as I knew it was gone. My poor nurse did not know what to do with me. She came into the waiting room to give me what she thought was good news. She said, "Your test is positive!" I said, "What does that mean? Positive is a relative term. Right now, to me, positive would mean I am not pregnant." My nurse said, "Well, positive here means you are pregnant." As I broke down crying, she ushered me into the doctor's office so that he could deal with me. When I walked in, he was doing paperwork and he slowly turned to me and asked, with a quizzical expression on his face, "What are you crying about?" I screeched, "I am pregnant!" He paused and blankly stared at me as he said, "I know." Between sobs, I managed to cough up, "My life is going to change drastically!" In his most matter-of-fact voice he said, "Yes, it is."

With that, I left my doctor's office, surrendered to the fact that things were going to change, whether I liked it or not, and that I needed a new plan. My new plan was to be pregnant, have the baby and head back to work as quickly as I could. However, nine months later, on February 25, 1999, I realized my plan needed to change yet again. Trey Alika Nakamura was born and I soon realized that I did not want to work the way I used to. The corporate ladder was no longer a priority for me. I was no longer willing to allow the daily grind of a commute to take away from my family time. The challenge was that I still needed to make an income to cover my portion of our family expenses.

As I thought through all of the income-producing possibilities, I remembered that I wrote a viable business plan for a training company during my master's program with a fellow student, Cindy Sakai. When we wrote the plan, it was just a project. We never thought we would do it. Now, however, it was the perfect fit for my lifestyle. Opening this business could afford me more time with my family while still making an income. I called Cindy and asked her if she wanted to do the business and as quickly as I asked, she said yes. Within a few months, we quit our jobs and opened our doors for business. This was the beginning of my career as a mom entrepreneur and training consultant.

Cindy and I began our journey in 2000, and along the way I have learned some useful strategies for growing a business while growing a family. This chapter will provide you with four key tips that helped me, and I hope they will be useful to you too.

1. Make family your priority.

2. You can have it all, just not all at once.

3. Make the world your office.

4. Be proud of your motherhood and never apologize for it.

Make Family Your Priority

Setting priorities early in the game is essential for making difficult business and family decisions. Cindy and I decided that our business would be scheduled around our families. All of our decisions are based on what is best for our families first and our business second. It is important to know that when we accept a client, the people there become family in our mind. This mindset is the foundation that allows us to provide exceptional customer service. It also makes us very selective in taking on a new client.

My husband and I needed to prioritize our own lives. This meant deciding whose career would have priority in our household. In the beginning, my husband and I tried to run our household with both of our jobs being equally important. Giving both careers equal weight created tremendous friction, arguments and just sheer exhaustion. We were both feeling misunderstood, underappreciated and torn in many different directions. Finally, I decided that his job would be the primary income and my business would generate supplemental income. This changed everything for me. My role went from being career woman and wife, in that order, to wife, mother and then business owner.

My husband is a loving and highly involved father. He is at every sporting practice, game, parent conference and school event. Making the children my priority just means that I make sure that the kids' schedules are taken care of and if I ever need help, I ask him for support. This has helped our marriage immensely because I no longer expect him to read my mind or think he should have known. Here is what we have agreed to: at the beginning of the month, I send him an email with all of the days and times I need him to take the kids to the bus, pick up the kids from school and be at a school event or practice. He puts the dates on his calendar and we are set. Yes, I do have last-minute requests. I just try to minimize the last-minute cries for help so we can keep a peaceful flow in the family. I believe that too many last-minute schedule changes is a sign of my poor time management and a sure way to create stress.

This does not mean that my business is not important. It simply means that Cindy and I only accept the amount of work we can handle with these priorities in place. The boundaries and priorities give me the clarity and courage to say no to some work if it does not fit our schedule. Managing the family is the priority; making money is secondary.

Here are two more ways in which knowing my priorities has helped me run my business: First, I rarely schedule training programs with my clients outside of school hours, and second, I almost never attend after-hours networking meetings.

Most people told me that scheduling myself like this would negatively impact my business. However, that is not true for us. We have experienced steady growth for 10 years. Could the business have grown more if I had worked longer hours? Maybe, and then I might be an entrepreneur who is also a mom, not a mom entrepreneur extraordinaire.

You Can Have It All, Just Not All At Once

I learned this early on. Do not try to parent and be a business owner at the exact same time. The end result is a stressed-out mother and a sloppy business owner. My suggestion is to work when it is work time and mother when it is mother time. Here is how I do it:

1. The early bird gets the worm. Often times I wake up at 4 a.m. and do all of my paperwork while the kids are sound asleep. When it is time to wake up the kids, I close the office door and do not look back until I get them off to school with hugs and kisses.

2. Parent time is parent time. There is work time in my house and then there is parent time. Before the kids were of school age, I would create a plan for the day, written on a dry erase board, and I would review it with them. A typical plan would show breakfast, mommy work time, lunch, family time, naptime and dinnertime. Work time for the boys meant they would do their puzzles, coloring, reading and so on, while I worked in the office. I always had space in my office for the kids to play, or they could be in their room. An agenda could look something like this:

AGENDA
7– 8 AM: Breakfast
8–11 AM: Mommy work time
11 AM–2 PM: Family time
2 PM – 3:30 PM: Nap/work time
3:30 PM – 8:00 PM: Family time
8:00 PM - ?: Finish up work

---

3. Now that my boys are of school age, I plan everything around their school schedules. When the kids are off, I am off and I do not feel guilty about it at all. When a client asks me for the day, I simply say, "I am sorry, that time is already booked." At first I feared that I would lose a client who I did not accommodate. I quickly realized that was a wrong assumption. As far as I know, I have never lost a client because of not fulfilling that first appointment request. We always find another time or day that works.

4. I consider my family time appointments as confirmed and immovable. This is important because many people have a tendency to move a family appointment for a revenue-generating appointment. However, a family appointment is priceless and once you start rescheduling family, it becomes easier and easier to do so to the point that you can become unreliable to your family. Does this mean I never move a family appointment? No. It just means that I think really hard before doing so. I want to make sure that it is really a necessary move, not just for convenience.

5. Always carry spare clothes in your car. Being a mom entrepreneur often means you need to be a quick-change artist. You need to be at a business meeting until noon and at a school event at 1 p.m. I always said if they sold black pants, a blouse and a pair of pumps at a drive-through, I would shop at that store regularly. Since mom entrepreneur drive-through shopping is not offered in Hawaii, I opt to carry a change of clothes for the entire family in my car. Some say this leads to a messy car; I say this is a sign of preparedness. We can go from school, to practice, to a dinner out, all out of the back of my mini-van.

Make the World Your Office

All I need to say here is *laptop* and *cell phone*. I do not think I have left the house without my laptop since 1999. When the kids were babies, I would take them out in their stroller and have my laptop in the bottom basket. Where most mothers keep their diapers and purse, I kept my laptop and file folders. When the kids were awake I would be talking with them, playing games and pointing at different interesting sights. The second they fell asleep, I would park my stroller, bust out my folders, laptop and cell phone, and start working.

Now that they have grown up, I have the same philosophy. I always have my laptop or iPad® with me. When there are a few moments of down time—for example, waiting for the kids to get out of school—I just bring out the laptop or iPad and tackle a few items of work. Every minute counts as a mom entrepreneur. Make sure you make the most of each minute and you will feel productive and accessible to your clients.

Summertime is a wonderful time to be a mom entrepreneur. I make sure to capitalize on this time together by creating wonderful adventures for us, some big and some small. Each summer we try to take a big trip to do summer school on the road. We spend our time studying history and geography as we travel to many different states. In fact, as I write this chapter, I am taking a month away from the office—still working from time to time—as I travel with my kids for a summer vacation in Washington, Canada, Alaska, Montana, Wyoming and Nevada. I am seeing the world with my kids and writing this chapter all at the same time. What did I say to my clients? I gave them plenty of notice that I would be taking the month of June off with my family. What do you think they said? "Sounds like a great time! Let's get together when you get back!"

Another tip if you decide to be absent from your office is to have a back-up person to be a main contact. For many years, Cindy and I took turns being on call for the business. However, as our business grew, we eventually hired a virtual assistant. Virtual assistants are inexpensive and a great support.

Be Proud of Your Motherhood and Never Apologize for It
This one took me awhile to figure out. In the beginning, I was fearful

of telling my clients that I was a mom entrepreneur. I thought people would not take my business or me seriously. In the early days, before my children were of school age, this was really difficult because clients would call and the baby would wake up unexpectedly from a nap crying, or the dog would start barking. Eventually, I decided to be straightforward with my clients. I told them I had a home-based business, that the children stayed home with me and were a part of my work world. My children quickly learned the rule that if mom was on the phone, they needed to wait to ask the question. I think it actually accelerated their writing skills because they would jot me notes while I was on the phone. Did I mention that you need to be a multi-tasker when you are a mom entrepreneur?

Our clients get to know our children very quickly since they often travel with us on business and take care of basic business tasks—answering the phone, delivering materials, setting up the classroom and so on. One day, I had a client who wanted to meet with me and I shared with her that while I wished I could, I had my three-year-old son with me for the day and I was unable to meet. What was her response? She asked me to bring him along and they had snacks and toys set up for him to play with while we had our meeting. I think it is valuable for the kids to see what work looks like, and that you can design a career that fits your dreams.

Being a mom entrepreneur has been one of the most wonderful blessings. I am able to spend a tremendous amount of time with my family and am able to show my children a different way of working and growing a business. It has been a journey with many surprises and I'm excited to see what other fabulous surprises life will bring to this accidental mom entrepreneur. Take note of all the ideas here that you think will make a difference for you as a mom entrepreneur as your extraordinary journey continues to unfold.

Sarah Kalicki-Nakamura, MAOM, CDC

Training Resultant and co-owner
TH!NK, LLC

(808) 224-6694
sarah@think-training.com
www.think-training.com

Sarah Kalicki-Nakamura is known in Hawaii for delivering personal development programs that help leaders create workplaces where people come to work because they want to, not have to. Sarah's upbeat style, fortified with meaningful tools, creates an environment where participants can explore new topics and find immediate results.

As co-owner of TH!NK, LLC since 2000, Sarah has experience working with a broad range of companies in the following industries: government, hospitality, telecommunications, automotive and healthcare.

Sarah holds a master of arts degree in organizational management from the University of Phoenix and a bachelor of arts in broadcast journalism from Arizona State University.

The most important roles that Sarah has are those of mother and wife. She is the proud mother of two delightful and energetic boys: Trey, age eleven and Wyatt, age seven. Sarah also has a wonderfully supportive husband, Malcolm, who is always quick to say, "Go for it" when she wants to start something new.

The Gifts in Being a Mom Entrepreneur

Unwrapping the Blessings within the Burdens

By Tara Kennedy-Kline, CDC, DCGL, MWP

When most of us think of a gift, we think of something wrapped up in a pretty package that we have always wanted and that will bring us joy and pleasure. Being a mom entrepreneur is indeed one of the most amazing gifts we can give to ourselves, and yet, as most mom entrepreneurs know, it can also bring to us gifts that are not always pretty or joyful—at least not initially. In fact, I believe being a mom entrepreneur is one of the hardest jobs on the planet, filled with numerous experiences and trials that may seem like incredible burdens when we encounter them. Yet when we take the time to look a bit deeper, dig a little further into the tissue paper, what we find are the true gifts—the hidden treasures that make it all worth the effort.

It is my passionate belief that there is a lesson in anything and everything that happens in our lives. It's about taking the difficult experiences, in our business or with our families, and saying, "Okay, this is happening for a reason. What can I take from it? How can I pull strength from it instead of allowing it to defeat me?"

That is how I finally chose to view my life—my life as wife, mother, entrepreneur, daughter, sister and friend, and all that comes with being every one of those at once. It has been a powerful and intense several years for me and I would like to share with you a bit about my journey, offering you steps to take along the way to assist you in finding the blessings within the burdens of your own life.

My Story

Between the years of 2002 to 2007, I began to believe that I was "plagued" by destiny. Over a very short period, life had thrown at me the five worst experiences a person can tolerate: debt, divorce, depression, death and diagnosis—"the dreaded Ds." Looking back, I now know that I was not really plagued because that would imply that I was a victim of my circumstances. I was not. Circumstances are merely situations in which we find ourselves—some of them we participate in the creation of and some of them we do not. Regardless of whether we help to create them or not, it is how we choose to deal with the circumstances in our life, how we respond and react to them, that determines how they affect us and those around us.

Although it was not always easy, I indeed discovered the hidden gems within each painful experience in my life. From debt I learned integrity; the threat of divorce taught me respectful communication; through depression I learned to surround myself with people who uplift me; from death I developed immense gratitude and from diagnosis I discovered how to find the brilliance in whatever was handed to me.

Though I am learning new skills and lessons every day, it was my journaling that helped me most through all that was going on in my life at that time. It is my experience that when we write, we release those things that are holding us back and we recognize the things that we are blessed to have. Writing can assist you in doing an internal inventory, reflecting on the decisions and choices you make each day. It allows you to be accountable for what you create, forgive yourself for your mistakes and acknowledge yourself for your successes. When you learn to hold yourself accountable, it's like strengthening your self-esteem muscle, which allows you to be stronger and wiser in the choices you make.

Cashing in on Integrity

To define integrity, most people would say it is the state of being whole and undivided. It is about being honest and living up to your highest moral standards. It is being congruent in your thoughts, words and actions.

While I was in debt and living with secrets and dishonesty about it, I was as far away from integrity as I have ever been. I felt that my life was a walking lie. I would spend all my precious time and energy trying to cover up or hide the financial burden I was creating—it was exhausting.

The pressure of it eventually brought me to my knees one night, as I found myself sobbing in the closet, crying out loud, "How can I stop this?" Soon after I heard in my head a statement of faith that simply said, "Bear the burden and make it right." That phrase became my greatest affirmation and ally in the days, months and years to come. From that point on, I was determined to focus on creating the solution to my situation instead of obsessing over the problem.

The blessing that came from all of this is that I learned clearly what it felt like to be out of integrity—with my family, with my friends, and most importantly, with myself. From this blessing, I was given the opportunity to step fully into my raw, honest truth, admitting my mistakes and then creating the opportunity to make them right. I learned the true meaning and experience of living a life of integrity and how empowering that is for all who encounter it.

Exercise. Think of areas in your life where you lack integrity in some way. It can be with your relationships, with your finances or in your professional life. Do you have an estranged relationship with someone with whom you want to make amends? Is there a daily practice that you have wanted to implement and haven't done it yet? Are there incompletions around your home that are causing you continual stress? See what comes to mind.

Next to each item, write out what it is you need to do to make it right. Is it to plan to meet your estranged friend? Is it to commit to a certain daily practice, no matter what? Is it to work on the house every Saturday for three hours? Next, add a date to each of the items that answers the question, "by when?" By when will you take the steps needed to be in integrity? Make sure the goals you set are realistic and accomplishable by you. Please remember that becoming fully aligned and in integrity is not an overnight thing. It takes time and patience. Be gentle with yourself.

Respectful Communication

Having respectful conversations means honoring the person with whom you are speaking and seeing them as worthy of the greatest care and respect. It means observing your words and thinking before you speak. It means listening with patience and presence as the other speaks.

Basically, for the first eight years of my marriage, respectful communication is exactly what my husband and I did not have. In fact, I would say we had the complete opposite. We were argumentative, hostile and hot-tempered. We constantly pointed the finger and blamed each other. During the time when I was hiding my debt from him, things were even worse. Every conversation would feel like a challenge or a fight, so we just stopped talking. It seemed to me that divorce was the only remaining option.

It was the innocence of a child that eventually made us realize that what we were doing was not working and that we needed to make a change. My then three-year-old son stopped us in the midst of a bickering session and asked, "Mommy, are you going to cry again today?" My husband and I looked silently at each other while we both considered what this child was teaching us. We needed to find a way to communicate that would set an example for our sons.

An important first step was to write notes or letters to each other instead of talking face-to-face about issues that we knew were sensitive. We worked on this daily and it eventually got to where our notes became love letters and the love letters became healthy, mature conversations. Growing this way together transformed our marriage and now, many say that they don't even recognize us as the same couple! It changed how we communicated with our sons as well.

Simple Tips on Respectful Communication

• Use "I" statements rather than "you" statements.

• Practice listening to the other person completely. Focus on hearing what the other person is saying versus planning what you are going to say next. After the other has said their last word, count to three in your head before you speak.

• Respect one another's opinions.

For further tips on respectful communications you can refer to my book, *Stop Raising Einstein: Discover the Unique Brilliance in Your Child and You*, published by Advantage Media Group in 2009.

Create Your Circle of Inspiration
Uplifting people are those who have a naturally elevating influence. Their very nature is to encourage and support those around them

to be the best they can be and uphold the other's greatness, even through difficult times.

During the period in my life when I felt completely lost and hopeless, I was saved from being swallowed by my depression when I began to seek out positive people to spend my time with. I noticed the friends I normally hung out with were actually pulling me down. As I started spending more time in positive company, it started to change the dynamics of who I was.

Now, the friends that I've reconnected with come to me if they're falling down, and they look to me to bring them up. We don't commiserate anymore. We talk about the great stories that celebrate our families and celebrate us.

Exercise. Make a list of those people with whom you spend a large portion of your time. This may include your family members, your friends and your co-workers. For each person ask yourself the question, "Does this person lift me up or bring me down?" Give a rating between one to ten, one being "not uplifting at all" and ten being "totally uplifting." Try to avoid the tendency to blame anyone for anything. Every relationship you have is co-created by you and the other person. If you discover some who are less than uplifting, use it as an opportunity to ask for what you want and need, remembering to use respectful communication. You have the tools.

The next step is, with that same list of people, rate *yourself* in regard to how uplifting you are to them. Use the same one-to-ten rating as above. Use this information to know yourself better and make changes where you see necessary. The most important thing is to honor and respect yourself and others in this process. It's all for the learning and the opportunity to grow.

Have a Grateful Heart

Gratitude is a quality of being thankful. It is having a humble heart. It is showing and expressing appreciation for the things we receive in life no matter what they may be. Yes, even if that something is losing someone you deeply love.

When my mom received her diagnosis of leukemia, it was one of the hardest facts I would ever have to accept in my life. I initially felt betrayed, punished and hopeless. I had recently lost my brother Jesse to a heart attack at only 19 years old and I wondered how much more I could endure. I soon realized it was one of those things that I could not change. The only way through it was to accept it—embrace what was before me and make the best of my time with her while she was still physically in my life.

One of the things that eased my heart was keeping a gratitude journal where I would write down all that I was grateful for every day, instead of focusing on all that I was losing. Through this process, I became aware of how amazing my life truly was and how lucky I was to have had so many wonderful years with my mother. It helped me accept the fact that my mother was here on this planet for a higher purpose than simply to bring me happiness. She had her own journey, outside of the pain and sadness I was feeling, and her illness and early death were a part of it.

Losing Mom and Jesse brought me the keen awareness of how precious and fragile life is. I realized how much greatness there truly was in my own life. This awareness certainly made me treasure my last months with my mother.

Exercise. Create a special gratitude journal for yourself. Every evening before you go to sleep, write down at least ten things that you are grateful for, either from that day or from your life.

At the end of each week, choose something from your list and make it a point to thank the person who made that gratitude possible. For example, if you are grateful to your husband for making you breakfast, find a special way to let him know how much you appreciate that about him. If you are grateful for your new car, write a short note to the person who sold it to you. You may be surprised how much deeper your gratitude goes when you share the blessing with others.

Finding the Brilliance

Finding the brilliance means to continually make the effort to find the higher purpose in every situation, event, person or thing that exists. It means trusting that there is a reason for everything and a gem to be discovered within.

Soon after my mother died, I was diagnosed with Adult ADD and my son was diagnosed with Asperger's Syndrome. Initially I was shocked—then I was angry. I cried and I denied. However, after all that I had been through, I knew this was just one more opportunity in my life to grow, learn, and find the brilliance within the blessing. I got to play the hide-and-seek game once again, searching desperately for the hidden treasures within the burdens.

It took some time, and eventually I found the brilliance in both of these diagnoses. I realized that I was who I was and where I was because of my condition, not in spite of it. The gifts of having ADD are that I am an amazing multi-tasker. I am highly creative. I can bring myself out of a bad mood easily because I am able to find the humor in so much. I am extremely efficient under pressure and if I am passionate about something, I can do it until I drop.

Many blessings were exposed by my son's diagnosis of Asperger's Syndrome. He is spontaneous, truthful and honest to a fault. He keeps us in check and accountable because he has the memory of an elephant. He is very literal. He does not tolerate or understand sarcasm, which has forced my husband and me to rethink how we speak to one another. Also, because of our own child's behavioral issues, my husband and I are not as quick to judge or criticize the actions of other children.

Once I embraced the unique brilliance that my son and I possess as a result of our diagnoses, I no longer felt afraid of them. I realized that all was well and exactly as it should be. Now we celebrate who we are, embracing the brilliance within the blessing.

Exercise. Take a piece of paper and make a list of the times in your life when you felt happy, successful, free-flowing or just plain proud. Keep writing until you feel like you can't write any more. Then go back and revisit the list, noting next to each event at least one uniquely brilliant thing about *you* that made that fabulous event possible. Was it your sense of humor, your organizational skills, your beautiful voice? Write as if you are making the list for someone you love. Let the brilliant gifts be revealed.

Next, on a separate piece of paper, write down some of the areas in your life in which you are seriously challenged to find the gift in the situation. Maybe it is an aspect of your marriage or your parenting; a situation within your work or with a friend. Maybe it is a battle with yourself—weight, habits, negative thoughts and so on. Now look at your list of what makes you unique and ask yourself which aspects of your brilliance you could deploy to solve or deal with that issue.

I believe our lives are filled with endless blessings. It only takes a little effort on our part to discover those gems. Do the above exercises and let me know what happens as a result. I wish you effortless success in finding the true gifts in every situation in your life as you continue to master your tremendous life as a brilliant mom and extraordinary entrepreneur!

Tara Kennedy-Kline,
CDC, DCGL, MWP

T.K.'s Toy Box

Dream • Play • Grow

(484) 824-2160

tara@tarakennedykline.com

www.tarakennedykline.com

Also known as The Multi Level Mom™, Tara Kennedy-Kline has always had a passion for business, family and dreaming big!

An entrepreneur from the age of 19, Tara has "been there, done that." During her 10+ years in direct sales, she excelled in her field, building teams of over 300 women and men with annual sales exceeding $1 million. Today, she owns T.K.'s Toy Box, an educational toy distributorship, which works with charitable and corporate giving programs. She is the author of *Stop Raising Einstein: Discover the Unique Brilliance in Your Child and You*, is a Certified Dream Coach®, and hosts her own radio show, *Straight Up Moms*. She is also an in-demand speaker and workshop presenter.

Tara is a proud supporter of Toys for Tots, Habitat for Humanity and Physicians for Peace, and is an advocate of positive parenting and providing unique education for spirited children.

Tara is truly dedicated to helping people find the unique brilliance in themselves as well as guiding them to set, stretch for and reach their highest goals, all while being present for their families.

Launch Your Business to Success

Build a Strong Foundation
for Your Business to Grow and Prosper
By Rhonda Johnson

Having your own business and being your own boss is one of the most gratifying, rewarding experiences you can have. You can set your own hours, make your own rules and experience total independence. It is also one of the most challenging, demanding things you can do. When it is your business, you are responsible for every activity from marketing to product development to customer service to administration. Everything rests on your shoulders. Despite this, I believe in the value of starting a home-based business, and I am going to show you the key tools for success.

I started my previous business, Accountable Solutions, a full-service accounting firm, more than 20 years ago. It became one of the fastest-growing firms serving the direct sales profession in all 50 states. I started my newest enterprise, Ignite Your Finances—Powered by Expense Tracker™, less than a year ago and it too is an amazing success. As you can see, I have successfully started and run two businesses. I encourage you to think of ways you can create multiple streams of income and leverage your activities in more than one area. Many successful entrepreneurs and mom entrepreneurs do this. When one source of income is slow, others flow!

In this chapter, I am going to share my expertise to help you reap the benefits and avoid the pitfalls of owning and running a business. I'll begin by helping you build a solid foundation so you can work your home-based business so that it pays, grows and prospers like any good business.

> *"I had to make my own living and my own opportunity!*
> *But I made it! Don't sit down and wait for the opportunities to*
> *come. Get up and make them!"*
> —Madam C. J. Walker, American businesswoman and pioneer of
> African-American hair care products and cosmetics

Start with a Compelling Vision

The first step in building a foundation for your business is to create a compelling vision. What do we mean by a vision? A vision is a statement of what you want your business to become in the future. Your vision needs to resonate with you emotionally and fill you with excitement so it motivates and inspires you, especially when you face challenges.

Your vision represents what you want your business to be. Use it daily to take action and make decisions. It helps you clearly define yourself in the marketplace and position yourself against your competition. It also helps you decide which vendors you partner with and where you market your services. It is one of the most important criteria you have for evaluating what to do and how to do it.

My vision for Ignite Your Finances is to be the number one educational provider for home-based businesses. A vision statement for a caterer might be: "To build a catering business that consistently provides perfectly prepared gourmet food, delivers outstanding service, and creates an extraordinary experience for clients." A vision statement for a wedding planner might be: "To become the premier wedding consultant for clients who want to spend more than $100,000 for their wedding."

Your vision is the first part of your foundation, and you can build more than one business on it. Look for ways to realize your vision in several areas. For example, if you want to be the premier provider of business communications in your area, you can achieve that through corporate writing, teaching business writing and managing outsourced organizational communications. In this way, you can develop many sources of income from your vision.

How do you form your vision? Start by daydreaming! It is that simple. Imagine what your business will look like and feel like five and ten years down the road. It can be a few sentences or several pages. You can write it as a story, or you can create a collage of images that capture what you want your business to be.

Pretend you are being interviewed for a magazine article. What kind of magazine is it? Who reads it? What will the article say about your business? What do you want readers of the magazine to know about your business?

When you attend your next high school or college reunion, how do you want to describe your business to old school friends you haven't seen in years? What would you say?

Your vision answers what your business will be in the future. It can include information about your ideal customers, profit goals, business environment and location, team, growth and so on. The more detail you include, the more compelling your vision. For more on creating your vision, see Sheri Cockrell's chapter on *Business Planning for the Serious Mom Entrepreneur* on page 57.

"Good business leaders create a vision, articulate the vision, passionately own the vision, and relentlessly drive it to completion."
—John "Jack" Welch, Jr., American author and business executive

Add a Motivating Mission Statement

Your business also needs a mission, which answers why you are in business. It describes your purpose and what your business does. It includes your motives and reasons for being in business, and like your vision, it motivates you. A strong mission statement can keep you going in challenging times and act as a daily reminder of why you started the business.

Create your mission statement by answering the question: Why do I have this particular business? Your mission statement can be simple or complex, as long as it sends a clear message about your purpose. It can include information about your products and services, customers, competition and so on. It needs to reflect what makes your business unique.

If you decide to have more than one source of income, you want to create a mission statement for each one. A business writer would have a mission statement for her corporate writing business and another for her training services.

My mission for Ignite Your Finances is to educate everyone in the value of having a home-based business and give them the tools they need for total success. A coach might have a mission statement like this: "My business guides entrepreneurs and small business owners in discovering who they are and inspires them to reach their full potential." For more on creating your mission statement, see Sheri Cockrell's chapter on *Business Planning for the Serious Mom Entrepreneur* on page 57.

"Nobody cares if you can't dance well. Just get up and dance.
Great dancers are not great because of their technique, they are
great because of their passion."
—Martha Graham, American choreographer

Communicate Your Vision and Mission

Post your vision and mission statements where you can see them daily. Everyone associated with your business—your family, team, partners, associates and vendors—should know what your vision and mission are. This helps them understand how they can support you in building a successful venture.

Make your vision and mission part of your brand and use it in all of your marketing materials, on your website, on your social networking sites and so on. Remember, your vision is where you are headed so you always want to focus on reaching that goal. Your mission is what you do day by day. Together, they are the foundation for business success. You must hold them so close that they become part of everything you do for your business.

When you are marketing different products or services to increase the number of income streams, you want to customize each with its own mission statement. One size does not fit all when you have multiple streams of income or more than one business.

Set SMART Goals

After you create a compelling vision and mission, you want to set SMART goals. George T. Doran, PhD, an expert in strategic planning, originated the concept of SMART goals in 1981. Arthur F. Miller and James A. Cunningham wrote about it in "How to Avoid Costly Job Mismatches," published in Volume 70, Issue 11 of the *Management Review* in November 1981. SMART is an acronym for:

- **Specific.** This means goals must contain detail and description.

- **Measurable.** Measures let you know when you have reached your goal and at what level of success.

- **Attainable.** You want to set goals that you can reach and that also motivate you to excel and grow.

- **Realistic.** This includes an ability to learn new skills.

- **Timely.** A goal is only a goal when it has a deadline.

A SMART goal for your business might be, "Six weeks from today, I will have a workable office space with the supplies and equipment I need for my first year in business." Another SMART goal might be "I will attend one networking meeting a week and meet at least five people at each event who can help me in my business."

Put your SMART goals in writing. In the book *What They Don't Teach You at Harvard Business School* by Mark McCormack, published by Bantam Books in 1986, the author writes about a study of students in the 1979 Harvard MBA program. The students were asked if they had set clear, written goals for their future and had made plans to accomplish them.

Only 3 percent of the students had done so, 13 percent had goals but not in writing, and 84 percent had no specific goals at all. Ten years later, the former students were again interviewed. The students who had written goals and plans were earning approximately ten times as much as all the other former students in the study put together! Written SMART goals help you succeed in business.

"One worthwhile task carried to a successful conclusion is worth half-a-hundred half-finished tasks."
—Malcolm S. Forbes, American publisher

For each source of income set short-term SMART goals for three, six and twelve months. Then, set mid-term SMART goals for three years, and long-term goals for five and ten years ahead. Break down these longer-term goals into smaller, short-term goals.

Keep your vision and mission statements in front of you as you set your goals. Review them regularly and take steps to achieve them. For example, if you want fifteen new customers within the first three months of your business, identify the specific steps you need to take to achieve this goal and make plans to take those steps. Remember, stay flexible and make changes to your goals as needed.

Implement Critical Success Strategies

Critical success strategies are necessary regardless of the type of business you have. You need time management and organizational strategies. This is especially important if you have multiple sources of income or are managing more than one business.

"Organizing is what you do before you do something, so that when you do it, it is not all mixed up."
—A. A. Milne, English author

Manage time to produce results. Begin to compare your current use of time to your SMART goals. Are you using your time most efficiently? Here are some action steps you can take to move you toward your goals.

- Use a calendar system. Life is too complicated to rely on memory. Properly using a good calendar system can add hours to your life.

The calendar is also a necessary tool to document business-related activities and expenses, such as meals with clients, meetings, travel and so on. Keep your calendars from year to year.

- Plan your day to support your goals, including some flexibility to allow for emergencies and last-minute changes. If you schedule your time too rigidly, you can create unnecessary additional stress when things go wrong and you have to juggle your plans.

- Make it a habit to do the most important activities first. Focus on your SMART goals. Knowing how to set and respect priorities is a mark of a good businessperson.

- Schedule creative or challenging activities for your peak hours— before 2 p.m. if you are a morning person, and after 2 p.m. if you are a night person.

- Stop procrastinating. Do it now. There are only 24 hours in a day. Time management starts with managing yourself. The more work and projects you put off, the less time you will have to do each. This often results in decreased quality and increased stress.

- Break up large tasks into small tasks and work on the small tasks consistently. Do not put it off just because you will not have enough time to finish the entire thing in one sitting. You can only eat an elephant one bite at a time.

- Do some work on assignments as soon as you get them. Do anything you can to get your mind focused on the project. This can provide momentum and help you move forward, even when you are not working on that specific project.

Use processes and systems to get and stay organized. Being organized is a habit. The goal is to automatically take care of things as they come up and implement processes for following up and keeping track of things. Getting organized and creating routines and standards for performing activities saves time and improves productivity. Here are some organizational and productivity tools you can use:

- Handle documents once. Do it, delegate it, diary it, discard it or file it.

- Establish a place for everything and keep everything in its place. According to experts in organization, people lose about an hour a day trying to find documents. Keep things neat.

- Set up a simple accounting system and open a bank account dedicated to your business to keep track of expenses and income.

- Empty inboxes daily. You lose time when you have to sort through documents you have already read. Never leave read documents in inboxes. Sometimes, you have to immediately respond to emails. However, time management and organization experts generally advise people to turn off their "you've got mail" notification. Instead, check and respond to email at designated times during the day, rather than when they arrive.

- Create templates for frequently used documents, such as invoices, standard contracts, fax cover sheets and purchase orders. Set up macros and auto text entries for frequently used phrases, such as your company's name, motto, tagline and so on.

- Learn how to use software efficiently. Some software lets you take phone messages and send them directly to the person's email address. Contact software helps you organize your phone directory electronically, keep track of calls and correspondence and remind you of appointments and the need for follow-up. You can use the merge feature to generate mass mailings that look and read like customized, personalized letters. Spreadsheet software can help you keep track of expenses, inventory, and other items that require analysis. Presentation software can add punch and pizzazz to overheads and slides.

- Keep your physical desktop and your computer desktop clear and neat. You should be able to sit down and immediately begin working on either one. Reduce the number of knickknacks, extra pens, pencils and clips. Do not stack files on your desk.

- Make it easy to work. If you are having problems getting things done, take a careful look at what is tripping you up. If something is awkward, difficult or disorganized, you will not do or use it. Keep things simple and usable—if possible, even fun—and you will work more efficiently and productively.

- Bundle similar activities. Avoid hopscotching from one activity to another. Instead, schedule times during the day to handle email, phone calls, copying and scanning, handling correspondence and so on. Performing a single activity for a period of time until it is completed creates focus and concentration. The activity goes faster and quality improves.

Start Now

"Twenty years from now you will be more disappointed by the things that you didn't do than by the ones you did do. So throw off the bowlines. Sail away from the safe harbor. Catch the trade winds in your sails. Explore. Dream. Discover."
—Mark Twain, American humorist and author

It is never too soon to start building a strong foundation from which to launch your business. Create your vision and mission statements, set SMART goals, install processes and systems that support you, and watch your business grow and prosper.

Rhonda Johnson

Ignite Your Finances

(949) 689-8714
rhonda@rhondakjohnson.com
www.igniteyourfinances.com

Rhonda Johnson is a uniquely qualified presenter whose insights on business management and taxation come from 34 years of direct sales and business ownership. A recognized tax expert, she has been interviewed many times by leading media, including appearances on ABC, CBS and MSNBC.

Rhonda's articles appear in numerous publications and she has shared the national stage with luminaries such as Dan Clark, John Gray, Brian Tracy and Hyrum W. Smith.

Author of four books, including the best-selling, *Making Tax A Game*, and Director of the Prosperity Center for the Direct Selling Women's Alliance, Rhonda has coached distributors in more than 160 direct sales companies to control their financial destiny. She is also a co-author of *Direct Selling Power*, published by PowerDynamics Publishing in 2010.

Rhonda's specialized business workshops provide your sales force with a solid foundation for success. Not only will she inspire them to take control of their finances, she will give them the knowledge, education and tools they need to succeed.

Business Planning for the Serious Mom Entrepreneur

By Sheri Cockrell

I am a mom and a business owner. I know that when you made the decision to go into business for yourself, it was for a very good reason and not made lightly. Whatever your reason, taking on the responsibilities of a business when you were already a full-time mom likely brought many demands and created many challenges. It was a courageous choice and I congratulate you! Disposable time is a resource that you have very little of now.

It is necessary that you utilize every precious minute to help bring balance to your life, which is one of your main challenges. Because mom entrepreneurs are so busy, they often do not take time for business planning. Know that if you take the time to plan your business, you will actually gain time.

Business planning is a critical time-saving and time-increasing tool. It will help you explore and clarify your business and create a direction that will build a solid foundation for a smoothly running enterprise.

Why Business Planning?

When your specific issues of time restrictions and interruptions interfere with business dealings, it can cause those on the other end to misunderstand your intentions. Many do not experience the same circumstances and cannot understand what you go through unless they are moms with businesses as well. They may not see you as a serious entrepreneur. The last thing that you want anyone to think is that your business is just a hobby.

Business planning will give you the credibility that you need to compete as a serious company in your field because you will intimately know your company and be able to work quickly. It polishes your knowledge and skills, stops time-wasting activities and breaks down intimidating tasks into distinct, doable steps. The added bonuses are defining your uniqueness as a business, and the confidence to be assertive. Also, you realize that you do not have to do and know it all! When applying this business planning system, you will become aware of the types of things you can delegate or the need for additional skills.

There are two main parts to the business planning process. Part One focuses on the heartfelt plan: the why, the vision, the mission statement, the goals and the objectives. This transitions you to Part Two, which is the working part of your business: analysis, strategic planning and implementation, decision-making, problem-solving and customer service. Let's get started now to make your business more successful and save you time.

Part One—The Heart of Your Business

The "why." Understanding your "why" for becoming a business owner is the starting point to really understanding your business. The reason behind your "why" will direct you toward your vision. Keep in mind that there is no right or wrong to your "why", and getting clear is important because it keeps you on track. Here are some examples:

- You are the sole income earner and need a second income stream, or you earn the second income for your family.

- You want a flexible working schedule.

- You want a better lifestyle for your family.

- Your family is number one, yet you do not want to wait to realize your dreams.

> *"Don't wait. The time will never be just right."*
> —Napoleon Hill, American author

The vision. The ability to put your "why" into a visual plan removes anxiety and agitation and replaces them with reassurance and composure. Ask yourself, "What do I want to accomplish with my business?" Maybe your product or service helps others feel better about themselves or their lives. Maybe it saves people time or makes their job easier.

Pinpointing your vision will also help you identify exactly what demographic your product will benefit. For example, the demographic for luxury products would be upper-income families with more expensive tastes. Economically priced products would be best suited for lower-to-middle-income families.

The mission statement. A mission statement includes the start-up belief and principles that your business will not bend from and keeps you on the same path after you grow. Creating a company mission statement helps you understand what your business stands for. What is your business's viewpoint on customer service, ethics, giving back, quality products and service?

Below is an example of a mission statement for a fictional store that offers clothing items for resale. The company follows through by providing staff and customer service guidelines. You can use this as a template to create your own mission statement and guidelines.

Mission statement for XYZ Boutique: "Our mission is to establish XYZ Boutique as the premier elite clothier for businesswomen while maintaining our firm standards of quality and affordability as we expand nationally."

The guidelines are established by you for your customers and staff to use to evaluate you and your business as it grows. These guidelines would normally follow directly from the mission statement above.

1. Establish an environment of respect and empowerment for all involved based on a philosophy of integrity and genuine caring.

2. Establish excellence in customer service by placing our customers' needs above our own.

3. Allow only top-quality levels of purchasing and operations.

4. Give back to our community through charity events and donations.

Goals and objectives. Setting goals and objectives will keep you focused on ways to bring revenue into your business. To utilize your time efficiently, I suggest that you set no more than three main goals per year—a three-month goal, a six-month goal and a one-year goal. Sharpen your goals into short, doable objectives so you do not become overwhelmed with unnecessary tasks and projects. I find that working backwards from my one-year goal is easiest. You may choose to work from your three-month goal and build. Do not be afraid to plan big, and never try to accomplish more than you can comfortably focus on. Here are some sample goals followed by objectives using our fictional company, XYZ Boutique, as an example of a start-up business.

One-year goal: Generate more cash flow.

Objective: To add $10,000 to my annual bottom line.

- Add Internet sales to our website.

- Add new clothing lines: sports and evening wear.

- Start promoting to a new customer base or market.

Six-month goal: Develop a large database of customers and potential customers, including new customer markets for sports and evening wear.

Objective: To promote and expose my business to more people.

- Create a website.

- Network and participate in local events.

- Gather contact information from potential customers to add to my database.

- Slowly incorporate new target groups for my expanded clothing lines.

Three-month goal: Get to know my business intimately.

Objective: To develop my business plan.

A business plan is an intimate, informal road map developed by you to use as an explanation of your business before and after start-up.

When developing your business plan, concentrate mostly on:

• Defining your target market

• Building your image and brand

• The ways in which your business and products are unique

Your image will depend on the type of business that you own and who your target market is.

Tips:

• Always ask for customer testimonials to help build credibility and trustworthiness.

• Work with a website designer to develop an outstanding website.

• Set new goals for the new year at the beginning of November of the present year. This is also a good time to reflect on which goals worked and which ones did not work in the past year.

Part Two—The Mind of Your Business

"A clear vision, backed by definite plans, gives you a tremendous feeling of confidence and personal power."
—Brian Tracy, American best-selling author
and professional speaker

Analysis. Analyzing, or dissecting, can work for you on both a personal and professional level. The system I use was developed by Albert S. Humphrey, a leader in business development, and is called the SWOT analysis technique. This stands for inner *strengths* and *weaknesses* and outer *opportunities* and *threats*. This technique allows you to evaluate every area of your business and know exactly when to take action and what action to take. Your SWOT analysis will be unique to your situation. Use the examples below as a guide.

Inner Strengths

• The ability to develop lasting business relationships

• The ability to plan activities for my children

Inner Weaknesses

• The inability to develop new product lines

• The inability to stop unnecessary interruptions during business hours

Outer Opportunities

• The closing of a competitor's business

• The opening of a new day care center near me

Outer Threats

• The opening of a competitor's business

• Added expenses for child care

As you acquire new skills, additional skilled personnel and team players, new product lines and deal with changing customer tastes, your SWOT analysis forecasts will also change. It is up to you to stay on top of these areas in your business to compete effectively in the marketplace and avoid stress in your personal life.

Strategic planning and implementation. The next step is to create detailed strategies and ways in which to implement those strategies to bring your vision, goals and objectives together and put them in motion. Find ways to create income streams that help your business grow and prosper by concentrating on ways to showcase your business and product.

Implementing your strategies involves taking what I call *now* action steps, such as renting booth space in local events that cater to your target market. Keep these flexible and short-term to allow for your specific "mom" situations or any changes in the market. Concentrate only on the events that can bring you clients who already have an interest in the product or service that you offer.

Have a Plan B that will allow you to respond quickly to situations by including team players in your strategies. Start a babysitting co-op with family and friends, hire your older children to help with tasks and give them a small salary, carpool to events, and so forth.

Choose networking groups that bring the biggest exposure to your business. This is a broader area to choose from because you are creating relationships based on who you meet face-to-face, as well as who they might know.

Take advantage of online social networking. It is a mom entrepreneur's best friend! Most of the events are free or can be accessed through the Internet and you do not have to leave the house.

The following two systems will help bring solutions to any problems or difficulties in both your personal and private life.

Decision-making. This is one of the toughest areas to conquer for any business owner, let alone a mom entrepreneur whose greatest emotional struggle is guilt. This guilt can cloud even the simplest solution and make the problem seem larger than life. When you face a difficult decision, you need to be able to come up with the best possible solution to the problem from several alternatives. The following six steps can take the emotion out of the process and allow you to take extra time to find a solution.

1. Identify and define your problem.

2. Gather all of the detailed information pertinent to your problem.

3. Come up with two or more alternative solutions.

4. Define the pros and cons for each solution. For example, one might be more expensive to implement than the other or one might take less time to achieve.

5. Take action on the solution that you have decided on. Don't look back.

6. Follow up. Did your decision result in the desired outcome?

I advised one of my clients to use the above process when she was deciding whether or not to expand her custom jewelry business out of her home. As a result, she is now located in a small storefront, with walk-in traffic and increased sales.

Fast problem-solving using the PMI system. You will not always have the time to solve a difficult situation using the above steps. In business, there are times when you have to come up with a solution fast. The PMI system—which stands for pluses, minuses and implications—takes your solution to any particular challenge or crisis and allows you the chance to see the consequences quickly and easily. Try this using the PMI layout below:

On a piece of paper, fill in the following statements below using a challenge that you may have recently experienced.

• Define the challenge.

• Identify the solution.

• List the pluses and minuses of your solution.

• List the implications or consequences.

• List the pros and cons of those implications.

• Confirm your solution and take action.

There will be times when it is impossible to make it all work in a harmonious way, no matter how hard you try. Sometimes you will need to take a break and come back refreshed in order to solve the issue.

Customer service. Your business's life blood is cash flow, and the way to reach and keep long-term customer loyalty is by building relationships through customer service excellence. Many mom entrepreneurs work in highly competitive industries such as jewelry, food and beauty. The need to stand out is a constant challenge. Here are ten recommendations for establishing excellent customer service and a unique edge:

1. Up your service excellence. Go one step above the service that your competition offers.

2. Never promise a customer something that you cannot deliver.

3. Do not waste time on projects that do not add to your cash flow.

You need to spend every available minute building quality customer relationships and making money to sustain and build your business.

4. You are unique. There is no one else like you. Use your uniqueness to set your business apart from the same business types and competitors in your marketplace.

5. Only market and promote to prospects who are in your target area and niche.

6. Develop creative ways to give personal, one-on-one service to your customers.

7. Give 100 percent focus to the task at hand. It is very hard not to want to be home when you are working, and working when you are home. However, you have to stop your mind from wandering. Instead, focus in order to prevent chaos.

8. Never say, "I don't know." Instead say, "I'm not sure. I will find out and get back to you."

9. Never say "if" or "maybe." Those lead to confusion and mistrust. Instead say, "I will," "I can" or "No, I cannot."

10. Never use foul, derogatory, or demeaning language in front of a client or customer. You are a professional. Always lead with integrity.

As with any planning, while details are important, avoid getting bogged down with particulars that just don't matter. Divide and prioritize your time. Apply the above principles to your business so that you are clear and focused. Doing this will routinely bring balance to your life and respect to your business, and save you time.

You Are a Natural at Business—Do Not Give Up!

As a mom, you are caring, open-minded and tolerant. You work easily on your own, and multi-task naturally because you have so much to accomplish in one day. You work well with others because that is what you teach your children to do. You are always learning and re-learning because you want to be a good role model for your children. You teach by example and experience. You instinctively nurture, which shows amazing support for others. You know when to take a stand, because tough love is part of the job. You are strong. Do you remember going through the birthing process? Please, no one is stronger. You sacrifice so that your children can shine. You forgive and forget. You are patient and see the natural abilities in others. You are tireless because your efforts build a better life for your family and you negotiate with the best daily.

Do not give up! Follow these ideas and delegate when necessary. Show the world that you are in fact a serious mom entrepreneur!

CEO

Women's Business Planning Service

Empower ~ Connect ~ Bloom™

(916) 782-5204

sher223@womensbusinessplanning.com

www.womensbusinessplanning.com

Sheri Cockrell ventured into the world of business ownership with her husband in 1994 and has owned a number of businesses. Growing into a self-made entrepreneur is not easy. Unless you take the right steps, you encounter many surprises and avoidable mistakes. Sheri has made it her mission to help busy women entrepreneurs by *empowering* them with business direction and skills, *connecting* them through bridges of opportunity and helping them *bloom* through affordable promotional events.

Based in Roseville, California, Sheri has earned many certificates of achievement and appreciation in business and volunteer work. Her faith-based principles and hands-on experience in all areas of business ownership help her clients save time and effort. A speaker, trainer and writer, she gives her clients leading-edge information and education in business and e-commerce to help them remain current with today's business transformations and environment. She is a proud member of eWomenNetwork, Placer Women's Network and the Roseville Chamber of Commerce. God's blessings.

Building Your Legacy by Thinking Big

By Teisha "Lady T" Shelby-Houston

Think big: to see beyond your current circumstances; to imagine the unlimited possibilities; to visualize grander opportunities and pursue them.

Your phone is ringing with business, the media is calling and your calendar is booked for several months out. You are the buzz in your city and you're even generating a stir on the Internet. This year's family vacation is completely paid for and so are all the bills. The children are strong and healthy. Thinking big is easy to do at this stage.

However, can you think big and see unlimited possibilities when you've worked hard for months and haven't yet recouped your expenses, when the opportunities trickle in at a snail's pace, when a virus has held your family hostage for several weeks, taxes are due and your spouse loses his job?

At the beginning stages of your business or when things are going your way, thinking big is not difficult. However, the day-to-day monotony of business and a few failures can definitely challenge your vision. Sometimes the failures can feel so severe they will cause vision blindness and amnesia, leaving you to wonder why you ever started a business in the first place.

Using the acronym LEGACY, I have mapped out six crucial steps to maintaining grand visions for your success. Indeed, thinking big naturally creates your legacy because you are consciously building who you are and having an effect on the people closest to you. Affecting those closest to you also affects the world. You can't think any bigger than that!

L = Live Like You're Dying

This is not to be morose, and it helps to give you a sense of urgency and a perspective that allows you to think bigger. While you have the privilege of living as a mortal being, you may as well play this game called life with great fun and expectation.

Here's an exciting activity. Think and plan out your funeral. Yes, take an evening to cuddle up with a journal and a bowl of popcorn and make your plans. Don't plan the morbid details, just the service itself. What are people saying about you? How crowded is the place? Are people sad with pity or sad with a sense of joy? Now think about what you *want* people to say about you and how you want them to feel about your passing away.

I want my "going home" service to be a family reunion, a celebration, and a motivating and inspirational service all rolled into one. I want people to be so grateful for how I have influenced their lives that they feel compelled to come from miles around to celebrate my life. I've already declared that flowers and sad songs will not be allowed, only balloons and uplifting gospel songs. The people who speak will be asked to tell their funniest recollections. What a grand time they will have!

In order to make that happen in the future, I have to plan to live a certain way now. You must also do the same. Thinking big means choosing your life's path, designing your business to have the greatest impact on people, sketching out your activities for a desired effect, being purposeful about raising your children and planning your success.

Write it out. Go ahead and write out what you want people to say about you at your funeral. Write out the adjectives that you want people to use when describing you. Next, write out the experiences that you want to have, the organizations that you want to join and what you want to be known for. Finally, list those who are closest to you and the impression that you want to leave on them. Remember that making an impact on just a few people greatly impacts the world!

E = Eliminate Fear

In order to go after the experiences that you need to create a grand business and life for yourself, you must eliminate fear. Fear is nothing but a mental construct. It is the mind's way of protecting you—really itself—from the unknown and its perceptions of past events. Unfortunately, it tends to exaggerate and over-analyze. Sometimes it will recite stories you've heard from the media and rewind scenes from the movies to fuel the fears.

Here are two secrets to eliminating fear:

- **Control what you hear and see.** Sometimes you have to be like the ostrich and stick your head in the sand. When the news of the month is lack, doom and gloom and you are working to see new opportunities for your business, you will have to withdraw from the media. The media is like mankind's collective mind. It pulls other people's stories from around the world, sometimes exaggerating, over-analyzing and generating the emotion of fear in us all. There are times when you have to decide to pull away from the negativity, stick your head in the sand and create the life that you want.

• **Take massive action.** This is the best way to eliminate fear. Jump right into those experiences you want, like going back to school, renting an office space, investing in an expensive program to learn more or even moving to another country. Your mind will remind you of your circumstances, your finances, your limited education and your childhood phobias. It will tell you that what you desire cannot be done. Remind your mind that you are creating a legacy and go for it! As American author Susan Jeffers has said, "Feel the fear and do it anyway."

G = Generate Your Own Momentum

So often we look to others for motivation and encouragement. External motivation will not carry you far. As a mom entrepreneur you must maintain a strength and fortitude that allows you to think big and carry on when your family and friends do not know how to support you, or your baby wants to be held 20 hours a day. What can you do to generate your momentum in the midst of trying times?

• **Affirmations.** Monitor your negative self-talk and write out positive statements that you can use to help change what you want changed. Recite these positive statements to yourself regularly until your brain is reprogrammed to believe them.

• **Vision board.** Cut out magazine pictures of the things you want to do and have, and the places you want to visit. Paste them onto a poster board or in a scrapbook and view them regularly. Use this to remind yourself why you are working so hard as a mom entrepreneur. My vision board is on the back of my bedroom door. On my most chaotic mommy days, I take a trip to my boudoir, close the door and relish the thought of my future safari trip in

Africa, my family's cross-country trip in the RV and the line of appreciative readers at my book signings.

- **Forgiveness.** Don't allow your past business mistakes to hold you hostage. Let them be your teacher. Every "wrong" investment, "poor" decision or "bad" timing instance is simply a lesson to be learned. Reflect, learn and quickly move on.

- **Business coach.** You may find yourself unable to determine your next move or you may feel unmotivated. Investing in a business coach is a proactive way of generating your own momentum. You'll have an objective partner, an extra set of eyes, someone to help you strategize and a person whose sole purpose is to help you prosper.

A = Action

Thinking big and building a legacy requires persistent action. Regardless of how things may look to you right now, you must keep moving forward. Susan B. Anthony appeared before every Congress from 1869 until she died in 1906, to ask for the passage of an amendment to the U.S. Constitution that would give women the right to vote. In 1877 she gathered 10,000 signatures from 26 states, but Congress dismissed them. In 1853 she gathered 28,000 signatures, but they were rejected by her state legislature because most of the signatures were from women and children.

Imagine the amount of work it took to collect thousands and thousands of signatures as a woman in the 1800s? There were no planes or cars to aid her transportation, no telemarketing, television or even radio to reach the masses. She was a woman walking or driving a horse and buggy in a hot petticoat, gathering signatures, generating a tribe.

She was arrested, beaten, insulted, ignored, starved, dismissed, laughed at and threatened and had other atrocities heaped upon her as she pursued her goals of legalizing women's rights. With very little encouragement or progress—it wasn't until 14 years after her death that the 19th Amendment was passed—she consistently acted on her dreams. She attended conventions even when she wasn't allowed to speak, she formed associations, she started her own publication, she established a press bureau, she met with presidents and did things that she knew would land her in jail again. Persistent action was her faith walk. She kept her vision in the forefront of her mind and continued to follow through.

You too must be persistent in your actions even when your dream seems impossible. Decide now that failure is not an option and take action steps every day, no matter how small they may seem. Believe in yourself, keep dreaming big dreams and keep moving forward!

C = Chart and Chase One Dream at a Time

All true entrepreneurs have at least 100 new ideas a day. It's very easy to flutter from one idea to the next, especially when the first one is not progressing as fast as you think it should. Keeping in mind your desire to make a significant impact on people, remember that you must first make an impact in your business.

Chart it. Chart out the plans for one business idea and make a decision on when and how you're going to release it. Maybe you will sell it after it makes a specific amount of money. Perhaps you will train your children in it and let them take it over. Maybe you want it to generate just a few hundred dollars a month and you'll easily let it go once your youngest starts school. You determine and chart out the steps you must take to make it happen. If you do not chart out what it is that you want, you will become de-motivated or confused when a new business idea captures your attention. This does not mean that you can't make adjustments along the way; in business you must be open and flexible. By charting and chasing one dream at a time you will become immune to The Shiny Object Syndrome.

The symptoms of this syndrome present as confusion, frustration, lack of patience and lack of passion. I strongly propose that you do what it takes to stay focused and enjoy the journey, no matter how long it takes.

Beautiful business ideas. Keep a list of your many business ideas. As a serious mom entrepreneur, you'll find that you are always open to what I call "the beautiful world of business-idea-butterflies." This world releases millions of beautiful business-idea-butterflies daily. They are playful and love to interact with entrepreneurs because they want to be manifested as a physical business in our world. A beautiful business idea will land on you and if you entertain it, it will release knowledge about how to help it metamorphose in your life.

Write it out. Some of those beautiful business ideas are just right for you, and they are not yet ready to be implemented. Those are the ones that you want to capture by recording them in a journal. Include all of the details. When it's time for them to be manifested, you will find that things in your world will automatically line up to support their manifestation. At that time, the window of opportunity may only be open for a short period of time, so I recommend you eliminate the fear and start taking action to generate momentum. If it feels too overwhelming, a business coach can help you prioritize and strategize your course of action. If you do not take action, the beautiful business-idea-butterflies will be released from you and go to another entrepreneur.

At the same time, not every beautiful business idea is meant for you to act on. Business ideas usually fly to me when I'm in the shower, sometimes two or three at a time. They used to overwhelm me because I assumed that I must entertain and implement them all. Now I know that they come to me because I'm an entrepreneur. I have learned to release those that don't align with my goals.

If the beautiful business idea is not in alignment with your plans, let it go with love. Don't fear. Hundreds more will be released tomorrow. Keep your eyes focused on accomplishing the current plan that you have already charted.

Y = You Define Success

I constantly remind my clients, ambitious women who once had thriving careers, that they may have to change their definition of success now that they are mom entrepreneurs. In our Western society we define success by money. In fact, we are conditioned to believe that a product or service is not worth much unless it has an expensive price tag. Many mom entrepreneurs have taken on the same mindset and have decided that they are not a success unless they are making a huge amount of money. I submit to you that success is relative and objective. Your definition of success should be determined by you—not anyone else. To create your own personal definition of success, you must be very conscious and keenly aware of your own values, interests, needs, desires and standards.

The old adage, "don't judge a person by where he is but by how far he has come," should be generously applied to mom entrepreneurs. Many of us are first generation entrepreneurs. Some of us have multiple children. You may have an autistic child, be taking care of your elderly parent, or dealing with your own illness. For some moms, just getting out of bed every morning is a success. Be kind to yourself when you look at your situation and do not let your bank account alone determine when you will declare yourself a success.

Write it out. Take time out to assess your personal definition of success. Living life on your own terms, going after your goals, raising happy, productive citizens, not letting success or failure go to your head, maintaining integrity, exercising regularly, having good health and an abundance of friends, having wisdom, influence and fulfillment, can all be used to measure success.

Visualizing the limitless opportunities and pursuing them was effortless when you launched your business. You can maintain your outlook and continue thinking big even during the challenging days of building your business if you remember you are also building a LEGACY. I wish you big dreams and even bigger success as you pursue your path of entrepreneurship while being a mom.

Teisha Shelby-Houston
"Lady T"

For You Who Have An Ear, LLC

(864) 990-7936
ladyt@thebusinesscoachformoms.com
www.thebusinesscoachformoms.com

Teisha Shelby-Houston (Lady T) charges moms to change the world through entrepreneurship and conscious parenting. Known as The Business Coach for Moms™, Lady T specializes in helping moms start, grow or transform their home-based businesses and themselves!

Because Lady T believes that "an empowered mom affects generations," she is proud to be the catalyst for other powerful women who have chosen entrepreneurship and motherhood. As a mom of five, recipient of The Woman of Excellence 2010 Award from The Church and Community of the UpState, and with a bachelor of arts in business management, Lady T is uniquely qualified to address the challenges of mom entrepreneurs.

She has been an invited guest on Oprah® and has changed the lives of thousands in organizations, seminars and retreats, and from pulpits around the world with her CAT-apult Coaching Program™ and her BlogTalkRadio show, *For Powerful Women Only.*

When Lady T is not tending to her husband or home schooling, chauffeuring or playing with her five rambunctious, very talkative children, you can find her trying to sleep.

Purposeful Profit

The Foundation for a Sustainable Business

By Audrey L. Godwin, CPA

"For where your treasure is, there will be your heart also."
—Bible, King James Version, Matthew 6:21

*T*here is an old business maxim that says the purpose of business is to create customers. For some entrepreneurs, that may hold true. For mom entrepreneurs, the purpose of creating your business is to make an impact on those people or causes dear to your heart.

While business management wisdom talks about the purpose of business, few speak to the purpose of profit. Profit is defined as having more income than expenses in a given period of time. However, when we talk about the lifetime of a business, the purpose of profit plays a more significant role. If you created your business to make an impact, then understanding the role profit plays makes the difference between doing the work you love and owning a job.

What is the purpose of profit? I believe that your business, in addition to meeting the needs of the people you serve, can also give you a significant return on your investment. Let's take this concept a step further. What if you could take the purpose of profit and give it a deeper meaning? What if you could have an impact on your circle of influence—family, friends, team members, vendors, suppliers and community—in a way that enhances their lives and gives your life deeper meaning as well? This is what I would call purposeful profit. Purposeful profit is the result of intentional action and stewardship of resources. It is the treasure that funds the desires of your heart.

As a mom entrepreneur, I imagine that you run your household based on the concept of purposeful profit already. You have visions and dreams for yourself and your family. You steward the resources you have to meet the needs of your family, funding and investing in the longer-term dreams and passions of each individual family member. Those skills can be easily transferred to creating and building a sustainable business.

When I coach clients to look at their business finances through the lens of purposeful profit, we apply the five P's—purpose, perspective, priority, plan and performance—to their company to shape the foundation of making their company sustainable.

Purpose

It is important that you understand the purpose of profit for your company. You may look at industry trends and other benchmarks. However, the bottom line is that you bring certain values and attributes to your industry just because of who you are. These values and attributes will guide how you use the additional resources that your profit will create. Answer these questions: If you own a start-up company, at what point in time will you make a profit? When you finally have a profit, what will you do with it? If you have been in business for a while, what do you do with your profit? Do you invest it back into the business through equipment purchases or increased marketing efforts? Do you increase your own compensation in order to take care of yourself or provide a longer vacation with the family?

Dr. Myles Munroe, purpose expert and business consultant, says "When purpose is not known, abuse is inevitable." I usually see that abuse in the form of having low profits in order to pay very little in taxes. Now, in the early years of a business, you may have losses or very low profits as you grow the business. I want to make sure you understand that whatever monies you are investing in the company are used specifically for the longer-term goal of bringing your vision to life and serving those whom you are meant to serve. I tell clients all the time that if they do not want to pay any taxes then they should not work.

Of course I am joking, and let's really think about this. The reason you went into business was not to pay the least amount of taxes. If you were working for an employer, would you turn down pay raises and promotions in order to pay the least amount of taxes? Of course not! Yet we seem to get into "letting the tail wag the dog" when we own our company. The purpose for which you created your company is unique to you, and you are inherently aware of what it is. I would guess that letting the tax man become the reason you have low profits and are contributing very little to sustaining your family is not what you really have in mind. I'll let you in on a little secret: one of my goals is to pay at least $500,000 in taxes. That way I'm probably making $1.5 million, which will allow my company to contribute to my family and the community in a meaningful way.

Dr. Munroe also states, "Purpose gives precision to life." The same is true for your company. Knowing your company's purpose in the marketplace, and what you will do with the profits you earn, will allow you to know with clarity what are true opportunities and what are distractions from the growth and profitability of your company. Knowing the purpose of your company *and* how you will invest the profits will help you create a sustainable business.

Perspective

Earlier I mentioned how I would like to contribute financially to my family and the community in a meaningful way. When I say *meaningful*, I mean from my family's or the community's perspective. The same goes for creating purposeful profit.

The perspective of the stakeholders in any company helps you shape the sustainability of that company. Who are the stakeholders? First and foremost, the owners; second, those you serve—your customers; third, your vendors and suppliers; and fourth, if you have them, team members. Keeping things in proper perspective allows you to create profits with integrity. These viewpoints help you know what necessary risks to take and investments to make for the short- and long-term profitability of your company.

I have a client who owns a roofing company. One of the core values the business is built on is service. They always want to be helping people. They had a customer who had some rotting plywood which the roofing crew uncovered when they tore off the old roof. Because the crew understood the company's core values, they replaced the rotting plywood at no additional cost to the customer. The result may be lower profits on that specific job. However, the customer became one of their biggest cheerleaders. If the customer is taken care of in a manner consistent with the company's core values, the company will replace lower job profits with an increased level of sales and customer loyalty overall.

I don't want to neglect the owner's perspective. Saying no to new business is also a way of creating purposeful profit. Will that new customer who has the potential to bring you higher profits be worth the near term sacrifice to your and your family's well-being? If you are not sure, then you may need to take some time to know the profit potential for your products and services. You may also want to revisit your original vision and purpose for your company. It is that perspective that keeps you going forward on those days when you want to lie down and take a nap with the kids—permanently.

Priority

Godfrey Davis, who wrote a biography about the Duke of Wellington, said, "I found an old account ledger that showed how the Duke spent his money. It was a far better clue to what he thought was really important than the reading of his letters or speeches." When it comes to your company's profitability, the same holds true. When we experience a net loss in a year in which we expected a profit—or vice versa—and we are surprised by either result, we have not been intentional in our spending or stewarding of the resources our company has generated. The people around us—family, team members, vendors and customers—will feel the impact when we are not intentional in aligning our finances with our priorities.

I share that brief story because purposeful profit requires you to have a sense of what is important as opposed to what is urgent. You need to ensure that how you spend your profits is in line with what you say is important. A growing company should be investing in marketing efforts. We are talking about a full-fledged marketing plan that outlines the target market—not just advertising. This plan would include strategies to determine where customers or prospects live, work and play, as well as the tactics employed to reach them. If you say that your team members are an important part of the company's sustainable success, then what are you spending on recruiting and retention? Do you have a budget set aside for their professional development? Do you offer a competitive benefit package? If you say that spending time with your children is important, then have you hired the team members needed to take on those tasks so that your time is freed up?

Knowing your company's priorities also helps you make clearer decisions when the pressure is on. For example, for managing cash flow, your priorities could be as simple as materials for income generation, team members, and then taxes. When cash is flowing, the order of payments is simple. When the cash is "dripping," then you can determine what will have to be paid first to keep everything moving forward. It becomes easier to have conversations with vendors to make payment arrangements when you are clear about the priorities of how and when to disburse cash.

The easiest way to determine the priority of your profits is to look at your financial statements. Your balance sheet will tell you what assets you own and how they were acquired—through debt or invested profits. Your income statement will show you the revenue you generated, the expenses you incurred to produce the revenue and the expenses you incurred for other items such as marketing, professional fees, rent, utilities and so on. Reading and under-standing these key financial statements helps you build or enhance your company's profitability.

Plan

Your financial statements also show you the results of your planning. This is an important aspect of your creation of purposeful profit, and Rhonda Johnson's chapter, *Launch Your Business to Success*, on page 45, will give you more insight into its creation. Also check out Sheri Cockrell's chapter, *Business Planning for the Serious Mom Entrepreneur* on page 57 for more information.

Stephen Shapiro, an innovation consultant and speaker, said that every business owner should have some level of competence in the four areas of the business:

1. Developing products and services

2. Generating demand for those products and services

3. Fulfilling demand for those products and services

4. Planning and managing the business

Of these areas of business competence, purposeful profitability hinges on the core competence of planning and managing the business. Your business plan does not have to be a voluminous document. It can be boiled down to one page. However, if you don't use your business plan regularly, then even the one-page document will look like too much work.

Having specific benchmarks in place to monitor, celebrate or tweak different aspects of your plan is vital to profitability and long-term sustainability. For example, if you decide that your company will pay 10 percent of net profits of a particular product to a specific charitable cause, you need to know if that product is creating a profit in the first place. Benchmarks are part of the planning process. For the clients I coach, it is imperative that they develop benchmarks for an entire year and review them every 90 days.

Let's go back to that example of donating 10 percent of net profits of a specific product or service to a charitable organization. Your accounting system has to have the ability to track that product's individual profitability. Another benchmark you may have could pertain to hiring another team member. You would need to know what level of sales would support another team member and the related equipment, space and benefits. Even if you decided to invest in a virtual team member, the benchmarks are the same.

There are four indicators that will help you grow your business in a way that serves you and your customers well.

1. You must know who your customers are and increase the number of customers of the type you want. A dear friend of mine,

Christopher Flett, CEO of Ghost CEO as well as an author and speaker, boiled down this step into two real questions: "Who do I serve and why does it matter?" Once you know why you matter to your customers from their point of view, you can plan on increasing your market share.

2. You must increase the number of times they buy from you. I prepare taxes in the winter, and in order to deepen the relationships with my clients, I also do business and financial coaching. If your business is seasonal, consider offering other products or services that complement your current lines. That way they can think of you all year round.

3. You need to increase the average value of the sale. Basically this comes down to pricing. Are your products and services priced correctly? Even in a tight market, people still spend money. Could you bundle products and services together in order to increase the average sale?

4. Last, and certainly not least, you must improve your company's processes. When do you bill for your services—when the project is complete or during your normal billing cycle? If you finished the project on the 3rd of the month and you bill on the 25th, there is a potential for lengthening the time you receive your payment. Speaking of payments, how is your collections process? Do you extend credit to every new customer? Do you call or email a few days before the invoice is due in order to ensure the check is in the mail? Do you accept credit card payments? Have you automated other processes in your company? Automating certain processes allows you the time and flexibility to focus your energy on those tasks where you alone bring value, like planning and managing the business.

Performance

Purposeful profit is a result of implementing and executing your purpose, perspective, priorities and plan. While monitoring your company's performance is important, watch out for ending up in analysis paralysis. Most entrepreneurs know intuitively whether or not they are going to hit a target. Set up time daily—early in the day—to list those tasks that must be completed to move your company forward.

Key performance indicators (KPIs) are more than just what shows up in your financial statements. They can be the number of customer calls you need to make in a day or a week. KPIs can be measured by the number of hours you spend in business development tasks, like visioning, strategic thinking and marketing. Another KPI measures efficiency by tracking how long it takes you to find a document, either in paper or electronic form. Other KPIs include your pricing and profit per product or service, meeting your target in 60 days instead of 90 days, or having the ability to plan for the next quarter or even the next year. Using industry-specific performance measures helps monitor the performance of your company as well.

Be creative in developing your performance measures. Measure your company's performance on what matters to you. Do you want to know how long your customers stay with you? Do you want to know what your warranty costs are? What about your returns or refunds? These are indicators that show how you are performing in the customer service area. Delivering products efficiently and with no damage is an operations performance measure. As a result of meeting or exceeding your key performance measures, you can celebrate with your team in a way that is most meaningful to you all.

As you can see, purposeful profit is more than having your finances in order. It is about committing to a plan of action that moves your business forward in a way that not only supports you and your family well, it also makes a sustainable impact on those you serve. Which of the five P's—purpose, perspective, priority, plan and performance—are you going to focus on next?

Audrey L. Godwin, CPA

The Godwin Group, PLLC
*Helping you create profits with purpose
by mastering your bottom line*

(425) 282-6915
agodwin@thegodwingroup.net
www.thegodwingroup.net

Audrey L. Godwin, CPA, has worked every job in the accounting industry from accounting clerk to chief financial officer. While she served clients in local CPA firms, she noticed a need for business owners to have financial analysis and strategic planning. She formed The Godwin Group in 2003 to bring this much-needed level of management experience to companies that have limited resources, yet need the expertise.

She uses her insight and experience to help business owners build profit and value through collaborative planning and implementation. She understands what drives business and how to turn reactionary transactions into strategic decisions. Her keynotes and seminars simplify complex material and make it highly user-friendly with down-to-earth tips, tools and techniques. She works with a wide range of clients, from start-ups to $5 million, to achieve financial goals that improve their businesses, which in turn enhance the quality of their lives and communities.

Her deepest desire is to see business owners understand their company finances so they are free to do the work they love and be financially available to make an impact on the world.

Branding: More Than a Buzz Word
By Tammy Tribble

*E*ntrepreneurs who are growing a business have all heard that they need to brand their product or service and are looking for branding experts to help them build and extend their brand. Most graphic design companies are now branding agencies. Branding is a big deal for a growing business, and what does it really mean? More importantly, what does it mean to you? How does branding help you grow your business and how does it make it easier to attract clients? What is the difference between branding your business and creating a logo? Where does it start? Where does it end? This chapter demystifies branding, providing clear and concise steps to creating a brand that speaks to you, your potential clients and your life!

What is branding?
The term "branding" literally comes from the cattle industry: branding a cow to identify the ranch to which it belongs. Branding cattle became a symbol of quality and consistency because the buyers knew which ranches produced the healthiest livestock and the best meat. Cattle buyers formed an emotional connection with their preferred brand through a continued relationship and positive dealings with the ranchers and a consistency in product and service.

The technical definition of branding is the identity of a specific product, service or business. It can be a name, sign, symbol, color, slogan or even sound. The reality is that branding is so much more; it is the emotional feeling a client associates with your mark. The emotion is based on a promise being delivered and an expectation of consistent value and worth. The client feels comfortable when purchasing a product or service from a familiar brand identity. It is this emotional connection to the client that is the foundation of your growing business, and the launching point for building a brand identity that has you stand out from the crowd.

Branding also benefits your business by adding value. Businesses with a strong brand can charge more for products and services than a competitor with an identical product or service that is not pro-fessionally branded. Having a strong brand legitimizes businesses and allows competition with more established companies. Also, branded businesses are typically more resilient in troubled economic times.

Your business is amazing and you have so much to offer. Now let's tell everyone by defining and communicating your brand.

How do you determine your brand?

Branding starts with the vision and spark that compelled you to start a business in the first place. It continues with defining your business and your ideal client, determining what makes you and your offer unique. Finally comes the visual representation of your brand that is needed to be competitive: logo, business cards, website, signage, brochure, advertising and anything else visual or auditory that you use to market your business.

Here are three important ingredients to assist your branding process.

1. Vision. It started when you put your heart and soul into starting your business. What did you want to accomplish when you started your business? What product or service do you offer and why is it worth your time and energy to share it with the world? What are your core values and beliefs and how did you incorporate them into your own business? What lifestyle are you enjoying as a result of your success? What emotions do you have when you talk about your business? How many people will you help with your business? What is your vision for the next year? Five years? Ten years? How do you see your business evolving and maturing? What other products or services do you imagine adding to your already-thriving business?

Take a few minutes and revisit the energy and excitement of launching your business. Write how that felt and how it feels now. Spend some time thinking about the future and envisioning success, growth, and the lifestyle your business will provide.

2. Definition. What is your business name and what do you do? Who do you serve and who would you like to serve? What do your ideal clients look like? Where are they located and to what organizations do they belong? How old are your ideal clients and why are you just right to meet their needs? What product or results do you provide? How are they different from others in the same industry? How are they similar? What makes you unique? What are the benefits of your product or service? What are people saying about your business? What are you doing that makes your clients come back to you and provide referrals? What do you say when you talk about your business?

Spend some time to answer these questions. Talk to your colleagues and see if they have any wisdom or input to add about your business. Talk to your clients and find out from them what value you bring. From this exercise you should be able to identify some keywords or values from which your brand will evolve. Maybe you value integrity and honesty, maybe great service and exceptional product. Perhaps you are committed, personable or results-oriented. My keywords for Mimetic Design Systems, Inc., include passion, integrity, positive, reliable, empowering and creative, and they all stem from the desire to help businesses be more successful.

3. Execution. Now we take the information you have and give you the tools to make your vision a reality. Your logo is the visual expression of your brand and should graphically capture the essence of your business. Your tagline should sum up what your business does, quickly and succinctly. The website is an extension of your brand and should convey your key ideas and concepts though dynamic, engaging visual communication and writing. The images and layout should all reinforce the feeling you are communicating and work to seamlessly communicate your message and perceived value to the user. Also know that you are an extension of your brand, and to be consistent with your brand you want to communicate your key message and values in your verbal and visual presentation.

Take a minute to look at your current business materials and personal presentation. Does everything you do, say and send out into the world support your keywords and mission for your business? Is your email written in a tone that matches your brand values? Do your brochure and website feel like they are from different companies or do they send out the unified message of business success?

> *"I've never felt like I was in the cookie business.*
> *I've always been in a feel good feeling business.*
> *My job is to sell joy. My job is to sell happiness.*
> *My job is to sell an experience."*
> —Debbi Fields, Mrs. Fields Bakeries®

One Message, Numerous Applications

Business Cards
Personal Presentation
Logo
Fax Cover Sheet
Voicemail
Letterhead   Signs
Email Signature
Website
Twitter®
Sales Sheet
LinkedIn®
You
Your Business
Your Brand
Products
Other Social Media
Facebook®
Bookmarks
Email Marketing
Print Publications
Blog
Brochure
Podcast   Video   Ads   Postcards
Speaker Sheet   Press Kit

What do you do next?

New Business: If you're a new business and just starting out, think and act now to set yourself up for the future. Start building your brand from the beginning as you move toward the vision you set for your business.

Susan started a legal recruiting business, Ytterberg and Associates, and hired me to brand her business, design and produce all her marketing materials, and develop an extremely high-functioning website. Susan wanted to be known as "the premier legal search and executive recruiting firm for legal professionals." She chose to invest up front in the kind of corporate design that would legitimize her business, give her credibility with new clients, and allow her to be a real competitor to much larger legal recruiting firms. She is experiencing great success and her vision is paying off!

Existing Businesses: If you have been in business for a while and have not yet put attention on your branding, now is the time. It is never too late to brand your business for success and be more effective as you share with the world your amazing products and services.

Ginny has an established image consulting business and wanted to take it to the next level. She hired a company to design her logo, and was unsatisfied with the results, ending up not using what was developed. She came to me frustrated and skeptical. We worked together to determine her brand and developed a look and feel that was just right for her. Once we had her new logo, we developed her website and her other marketing materials. Because she has co-authored several books, we even designed bookmarks for her. She is on the road to success and has even had some television appearances as a result of her consistent and professional branding. You see, it is truly never too late to upgrade your existing business brand.

How do you hire a graphic designer or design firm?

The most important thing in the branding process is to hire a graphic designer or design firm to brand your business and develop a professional logo and all your marketing materials. Do not make the mistake of letting a family member with a laptop design your logo or build your website. Would you let an energetic student who tinkers with a go-cart work on the brakes of your car? No! The same is true for graphic design. Designers are trained in branding, typography, contrast, the psychology of color, scale, spacing and much more. The right graphic designer could be one of the most valuable people on your business success team.

You know you need a professional to brand your business and set the stage for success, and hiring a design professional can be scary and feel risky. Here are a few tips that could simplify the process and help you find someone who is right for you and your business:

- Start looking at other people's business cards and websites and ask them if they would recommend their graphic designer. If you are working with a business coach or consultant, find out who that person recommends. Ask your colleagues about their experience and find out if they feel they got a great value.

- When you are investigating possible designers, look at their portfolio and ask for samples of work that relate to your business or industry.

- Ask the designer if you could contact some of his or her previous clients. Call them and find out about their experience.

- Interview the designer or main contact at the firm. If that person is unwilling to spend some time now, then it will probably not be a great match later.

- Listen to the questions they ask. Are they interested in your business and finding out about you? Are they asking about your mission, your ideal client, and plans for the future of your business? Are they good communicators?

- Find out about their process and what happens should you not get a logo or product that you feel is right for your business. Ask to see a typical project and look at presentations from beginning to end. Ask how many revisions you get on a logo or other materials.

- Find out if they can meet all your needs—not only your logo—also your website and other marketing materials.

- Ask yourself if it feels right working with this person or firm. Are you excited about getting started? Are you eager to pay the deposit?

Your intuition is key here and clients who go with their instincts are more likely to get a great product and fantastic brand.

What can you expect when working with a designer?

While every designer has his or her own way of doing things, the overall process is quite similar within the design industry.

• The process starts with an interview. Most of the time this takes about an hour. This is where designers learn about you and your business and develop a strategy for creating your brand.

• Some firms ask the client for samples of logos or sites they like and what they like about them. This sets the stage for success and the designer learns the client's visual vocabulary. I find this to be a key component in developing a successful logo and brand.

• Most firms allow for three rounds of revisions in the logo process. This is a personal choice of the designer or firm. I usually do not have more than three, and I will continue to work until the client is satisfied.

• At the end of the process, most firms give clients print-ready files to get their business cards or brochure printed. Most supply a CD with all logos and files for the client to use as needed.

• Printing is typically not included. Most firms have printers they recommend and on some projects the estimate may include press supervision. This is above normal design and production and usually costs extra.

• On websites, the production of a site is usually included and the estimate will include backend programming and launching the site. Make sure to ask if all of this is included in the estimate.

• Proofreading and copywriting are always extra. Some firms have a copywriter on staff and usually have a recommendation for a proofreader. You can often have the designer handle both. Ask for those steps to be included in the estimate. I always recommend proofing.

• Payment is usually collected in two to three payments, depending on the size of the project. There is always a deposit required; the second payment is commonly due on design approval, with the final payment due before release of the files or launch of the site.

• An agreement is often a good idea. Some designers have a standard contract and others use an email agreement. This helps make sure everything agreed upon is provided.

Branding is one of the most important undertakings of any growing or thriving business. Enjoy the process and discover the key elements and values that are distinctive for your business. Set yourself up for growth. Remember that your business is amazing and you have so much to offer. Commit to taking action to brand your business for success and make your vision a reality!

Tammy Tribble

Mimetic Design Systems, Inc.

Making the vision a reality

(510) 881-8446
tammyt@mimeticdesign.com
www.mimeticdesign.com

Tammy Tribble is the founder and creative director of Mimetic Design Systems, Inc. She graduated with honors from California College of the Arts with a bachelor of fine arts in graphic design, and has been self-employed since 1999. After her daughter was born in 2004, she became an official mom entrepreneur.

For Tammy, being a graphic designer is so much more than designing a logo, brochure or website. It is about helping her clients fulfill their dreams. As a member of their success team, Tammy asks pertinent questions that clearly define their short- and long-term goals. She makes suggestions, provides input and often writes the copy for her clients. She is totally committed to the client's satisfaction and will do what it takes to make sure the project meets or exceeds their expectations. She looks at the big picture and helps the client envision the possibilities while she provides the tools to make that vision a reality.

Tammy provides the best in corporate graphics for emerging and growing businesses all over North America. She has worked with some amazing entrepreneurs and mom entrepreneurs, and her business has prospered through referrals and client loyalty.

Turn Your Image into Gold

Cultivate an Image to Support Your Professional Goals

By Jennifer Bressie

"Style is a magic wand,
and it turns everything to gold that it touches."
—Logan Pearsall Smith, American writer

Roger Ailes, a media strategist, famously said, "You have just seven seconds to make a good first impression." Your image is critical, no matter what area of business you pursue. It communicates your success, your attention to detail, your ability to stay current and your level of self-respect—without you saying a word. When you cultivate an image that supports your business goals, you can turn that image into gold.

When your dress is inconsistent with your professional role, people become confused—or worse, they question your expertise. If you went to a five-star restaurant and met the chef, you would be less than impressed if he came out wearing a messy, faded T-shirt, old grungy sweatpants and dirty sneakers. He would not look like the expert you were anticipating. Clothing communicates roles and levels of expertise that people interpret as credibility. Dress the part for the role you want to play, and people will buy what you are selling!

"Dress shabbily, they notice the dress.
Dress impeccably, they notice the woman."
—Coco Chanel, French fashion designer

Cultivate Your Image

My business began when my children were all school-aged. I was looking for a way to pursue my passion while having the flexibility to spend time with my children. My first clients were friends or women I knew in the community who, like me, were mom entrepreneurs. Together, we found that reinventing ourselves as experts was an integral part of building our businesses.

Think about your current personal image. Are you wearing clothes better suited to your life as a stay-at-home mom or from your career before you had children? What would better represent your life, lifestyle and career right now? Building a business is a rewarding, exciting choice. Make sure you give your business all the advantages you can by ensuring your image is an accurate reflection of your message.

Often, when I describe my job, people assume I work with very wealthy clientele, such as politicians or celebrities, because they believe image is something only famous, glamorous people worry about. In fact, most of us—from business executives to stay-at-home moms to recent college graduates—need to take stock of our personal image.

Many things in your life need check-ups. Your children get annual medical exams, your car gets a regular tune-up, and your image needs to be assessed every few years as well. When you take care of your image, you will never be overlooked, you will be taken seriously and you will gain opportunities due to your perceived expertise. You will also gain confidence and a healthy self-esteem because you have a polished image.

How do you create an image that supports your goals and aspirations? This chapter will give you a great head start on the process. If you are finding it difficult to tackle your image on your own, an image professional can help. A good consultant is skilled in understanding the messages of specific clothing details, colors, textures and styles. She can also work within any budget to help you achieve your goals.

"Vision without action is a daydream.
Action without vision is a nightmare."
—Japanese proverb

Focus on Your Message

Wherever you are in the process of becoming a mom entrepreneur extraordinaire, you need to focus on your message. Depending on the type of company you are building, determine the appropriate message that will support your goals.

My friend and client, Betsy, is a master gardener. She has a successful container garden and landscaping business. When she is working for a client, Betsy wears cotton khaki pants and a green, collared shirt on which she has had her company logo printed . The uniform Betsy has established always makes her look professional, neat, and like an expert in her field. In addition to its appearance, and its being perfect for her business goals, her uniform is inexpensive, easy to clean and job-appropriate. Here are some questions to help you focus on your message:

• What is your message? Can you state it in 25 words or less?

• How do you wish others to perceive you?

• What are some appropriate adjectives with which you would like to be described?

103

Here are some possible adjectives to get you started:

appropriate	artistic
athletic	authorative
avant-garde	beautiful
bold	capable
carefree	composed
confident	credible
cute	daring
dedicated	delicate
dependable	dignified
direct	dramatic
dynamic	elegant
energetic	exciting
fun	hip
innovative	organized
original	outrageous
playful	poised
polished	powerful
relaxed	reserved
serene	sophisticated
striking	unique
unusual	

Of course, this is a preliminary list. Feel free to branch out and think of some of your own. There are even classes available on the language of clothing and image. Ask a friend or an image consultant to help you with this if it is difficult for you to do on your own.

I recommend you start a fashion notebook or binder where you can make lists of goals, fashion ideas and so on. Right now, take a moment to think about some messages you would like to convey with your image. Make a list in your notebook.

Begin to pull from catalogs or current magazines pages that support the message you would like to create and include these in your fashion notebook. Take your time. It may take weeks, or even months, to find images, words and pictures that truly represent your personal style. Once you have a good stack of pictures, look for common threads or themes, such as artistic, classic or modern. Are there any recurring colors? Did you pull photos of bags, shoes and jewelry? Like fashion runways, fashion magazines can feature some wild variations on current trends. Try to isolate details that resonate with you without being bogged down by "I-would-never-wear-*that*-outfit!" resistance. Tear out anything that draws you, whether it is the style, color, pattern or feeling it gives you.

Comparing and contrasting is a great way to determine whether or not your wardrobe and image are where they need to be. One way to do this is to do an exercise I call "Past/Present." On a separate sheet of paper, complete the following sentences, defining the things that have changed or evolved in your life. Feel free to include as many items as you think applicable.

• "In the past, I _____.

• Moving forward, I would rather _____."

Here are some examples:

In the past, I had a closet full of clothes which all looked the same. Moving forward, I would rather purchase fewer items that are more distinctive.

In the past, I wore suits and heels every day. Moving forward, I would rather wear clothes that are comfortable and flowing.

In the past, I would rummage through my closet every morning, ultimately leaving for work looking the same as yesterday, with a pile of clothes to clean up when I got home. Moving forward, I would rather have a clean, organized closet that makes getting dressed fun and easy.

In the past, I wore baggy jeans and practical shoes. Moving forward, I would rather have a more polished, put-together and professional look.

> *"In order to seek one's direction, one must simplify the mechanics of ordinary everyday life."*
> —Plato, Greek philosopher

Align Your Wardrobe with Your Life Changes

When your life changes, your clothes have to change with it. One way to tackle your wardrobe needs is to list the various roles that make up your lifestyle. Take a minute to think about the different roles you play—entrepreneur, mother, partner, athlete, volunteer and so on. Then, think about the activities that are involved in carrying out each role, such as networking, carpooling, date nights, tennis matches and so on. One role may involve several activities.

On a separate sheet of paper, list the top four roles in your life. Beneath each, list at least three activities that go along with that role. Here is an example:

Role: Mother
Activities:

• Errands

• Attend children's sporting events and activities

• Casual family dinners out

Assign a percentage value for the amount of time you spend on each activity. Your wardrobe needs should correlate to that percentage. Also, if you are working 40 percent of the time, at least 40 percent of your wardrobe should be made up of clothing appropriate for working. Understanding your roles and the related activities helps determine what clothes you need.

> *"True elegance consists not in having a closet*
> *bursting with clothes, but rather a few*
> *well-chosen numbers in which one feels totally at ease."*
> —Coco Chanel, French fashion designer

Before you assess your wardrobe needs, you might want to do a quick cleanout and straighten up what you already have. Follow these simple steps and say "hello" to the closet you have always dreamed of—organized, functional, full of clothes that flatter you. Create an inspirational space where you will enjoy getting dressed each day. If this terrifies you, think about enlisting the help of a professional.

Step One: De-Clutter

Is there obvious clutter you can get rid of quickly? Here are a few items I frequently find in closets:

• Plastic dry cleaners' bags, which are very bad for your clothes. Fabrics like to breathe.

• Scores of mismatched hangers. Matching hangers make the closet look uniform, allowing your eye to focus on the garments rather than being distracted by the different sizes and types of hangers. Wooden or bamboo hangers are particularly excellent for helping jackets maintain their shape.

• Empty shoe boxes.

- Non-wardrobe items such as sports equipment, boxes of photos, art project materials and so on.

Start by setting a timer for 15 minutes. Take out a big trash bag, remove non-wardrobe items from your closet, and dump the clutter.

Step Two: Do a Seasonal Swap

When working with clients, I recommend they keep only the current season's clothes in their closet. Change your closet twice a year, in the fall and in the spring. It usually works well to change the closet when you change the clocks for daylight savings time. Doing this makes it easier to see what you have to wear that is seasonally appropriate. There are many storage solutions for your off-season clothes, such as plastic bins, hanging canvas bags or under-bed storage. These are valuable tools for closet management.

I once visited a client who told me she had lots of color in her closet. Yet she had difficulty figuring out what to wear or how to pair things together. Since it was winter, we first removed all the spring and summer clothes. She quickly discovered she had only black, grey and navy in her winter wardrobe. No wonder she couldn't figure out how to pair her colored items, since most of her colored clothing was off-season. She needed to add some beautiful, colorful cashmere sweaters or scarves to brighten up her winter clothing.

Now, for the real challenge!

Step Three: Let It Go

Once you have removed the clutter and your off-season items are packed away, assess what is left. Go through everything. The only clothes that will *stay* in your closet are the ones that fit, flatter and complement your style. To help you decide what will stay and what will go, ask the following questions:

- Would I buy it again at full price?

- Does this reflect the adjectives with which I would like to be described?

- Is this ill-fitting garment worth keeping and altering to fit me, or should I just go buy a new one?

- Does this look overly worn?

- Is this appropriate for the career I now have?

Anything that gets a "Hmmm" or a "But I loved this in college" response gets put aside for charity or a consignment store. You will feel fantastic about letting those items move on to help another.

Now you have a closet full of clothes that reflect your personal style and resonate with the message you wish to convey about you and your company. It is time to get organized for quick and easy access. Head to a store like Target®, The Container Store® or Bed Bath & Beyond® and purchase organizing containers. Here are some suggestions:

- **Shoe racks.** There are many options, and some even hold boots. Choose one that works for your space.

- **Canvas clothing bags** to hold items used infrequently.

- **Drawer dividers** to separate your underwear from your socks and so on.

- **Jewelry boxes** to help you sort out jewelry.

When your clothes and accessories are neatly organized and visible, you will reach for them and use them more.

> *"We are shaped and fashioned by what we love."*
> —Johann Wolfgang van Goethe, German writer

Look for current fashion trends in your closet. Fashion designers and magazine editors may be wild for the military look this season, and you do not have to buy camouflage leggings, six-inch platform military boots or expensive leather jackets with epaulet detail to show you are "with it." You just need to hint at the trend to look current. Check your closet; you might find some khaki green items that will work. Maybe you have a cute jacket with some brass buttons or a pretty blouse with shoulder epaulets. Work with what you have and avoid investing in expensive, short-lived trends. Once you have found your trend pieces, start to make some outfits. Try putting a straight-leg pant and a simple neutral T-shirt together with a trendy military jacket and belt to create a sophisticated, adventurous look.

Mix and match your favorite pieces to make fresh, new outfits. Do not forget about accessories! A great handbag or a fantastic chunky necklace can pull the whole look together. Go back to your magazine images, study the looks and repeat them using your own accessories. Write down these new combinations in your new fashion notebook so you can replicate them in the future.

Congratulations! You have just completed the quick version of an image makeover. If you continue to follow these simple steps and regularly give your image a check-up, it will never be a liability, and always an asset. You can breathe new life into your wardrobe and capitalize on the investment hanging in your closet. Once you make the commitment to manage your image, you can focus your energy on building your successful business. Reap the rewards of your investment, celebrate your success and move forward with confidence and style. Start now to follow these easy steps to turn your image into gold.

Jennifer Bressie

Image and Style Consultant

(650) 867-5399
jennifer@jenniferbressie.com
www.jenniferbressie.com

Jennifer is a trusted image and style consultant based in the San Francisco Bay area. With over 20 years of expertise in fashion, she is known for her ability to guide her clients through the development of their personal style. She is a dedicated closet clutter eliminator and believes that above all else, getting dressed should be fun. She is totally committed to assisting her clients to achieve that joy.

Jennifer serves a diverse group of clients, including women, men, teens and children. Privately, she assists her clients with body and style analysis, closet audits, personal shopping and wardrobe management. She is known to be quite helpful to spouses with gift giving as well.

As a dynamic speaker, she has led workshops, and presented to professional organizations and volunteer groups on various aspects of image, including accessory selection, style definition and closet clearing. She is an Associate Member of Color Designers International and is an active member of the Association of Image Consultants International.

Jennifer looks for fun and joy in all that she tackles and she brings this joyful spirit to working with her clients.

The Art of Leveraging Your Time

The Mom Entrepreneur's
Key to Blending Career and Family
By Martha Staley, CDC

"If you want to make good use of your time, you've got to know what's most important and then give it all you've got."
—Lee Iacocca, American corporate executive

As a mom entrepreneur, you have chosen and created a work-from-home opportunity. You have decided to establish a business that will allow you to be available full-time for your family and at the same time, fulfill your financial and career goals. You want to have it all.

Like you, I believe that you can have it all—your personal, family and business dreams, and the success that you desire. The best place to begin your journey is by clarifying where, when and how you will master the 24 hours in every day that you are given.

The two biggest challenges a mom entrepreneur faces on a daily basis are how to balance the requirements of her family with those of her business and how to leverage her time to maximize the available hours in her day. This chapter can be your road map as you discover strategies to help you solve these challenges.

You will discover some work-from-home business strategies that will make it easier to blend your family and your business life together, and you will acquire some techniques for mastering the art of leveraging your time. As a result, you can be more effective and productive in your business and have more quality time for your family.

Establishing Ground Rules for Your Work-from-Home Business

Here are three ground rules that will help incorporate your business into your family and create a solid foundation for success:

1. Have a clear business vision and get your family's support. A crucial step to achieving the business of your dreams is to have a clear picture of what it looks like, develop a business plan to achieve it, and gather the support of those who will cheer you on as you progress. To determine your business vision, ask yourself these questions:

- Why did I decide to become a mom entrepreneur?

- What are the results that I want to achieve by having a work-from-home business?

- What are the necessary elements that absolutely have to be in place to make my vision blend with my personal and family values and priorities?

- What am I willing to do or to give up that will make my vision my reality?

Once you have written your business vision, share it with your family, let them know how they can help you and ask for their support.

My client Michelle shared with me that she didn't realize how having a business vision could make such a huge difference in her business until she created one and asked her family to be an integral part of her support team. Within a few weeks, she acknowledged that her family was more encouraging and helpful, and that her daily business expectations were beginning to be realized much faster because of her family's understanding and support.

2. Have a personalized time management system. Your days are not one-size-fits-all. Based on your unique circumstances, values, principles and priorities, your schedule is different from that of most other people. Find a planner that is flexible, that you can personalize, and that will adapt to your ever-changing world on a daily basis. There are two systems I recommend. One is My Calendar and Time Mastery System and the other is a web-based system called Time Champ™ at www.timechamp.com.

When I first met Karen, she was extremely frustrated. Daily interruptions kept her from staying focused and there were many days that she failed to accomplish tasks because she was waiting for the perfect time. Once we created a personalized time management system for her, centered on her personal life circumstances, family and business, she was amazed how easy it was to complete the necessary business activities and have the time she desired to spend with her family too.

3. Set office hours and keep them. As a person who works from home, one of the hardest things to do is to keep office hours. It is so easy for people, household tasks and everyday life to interrupt you. People may think that what you do is not a "real" job. As a result, you may find yourself agreeing to do a favor or taking a phone call that will keep you from moving forward toward achieving your daily goals.

Because household tasks are always visible when you work from home, they can easily cause daily distractions. The thought might be that it only takes a few minutes to put laundry in the washer, for instance. On your way, however, you get sidetracked and think of something else you need to do. Before you know it, an hour or two has passed before you return to your office.

Determine your office hours based on your business vision, what is best for you and what is best for your family. As someone who is building a business around her family priorities, your office hours could change from day to day. Having a flexible schedule is one of the perks of being a mom entrepreneur.

Even though they may change from day to day, by scheduling office hours and making the commitment to adhere to them, you are exhibiting to yourself and others that you are serious about what you do. As for the laundry and other tasks that have nothing to do with your business vision, be sure to delegate them or block off another time for them to be accomplished.

Leverage Your Time by Incorporating Time Expanders into Your Day

Here are several advantageous time expanders to consider:

Effective planning of your time. To effectively leverage your time and set yourself up for success, block off specific planning time for your daily, weekly and monthly schedule.

An exercise that can be very beneficial is tracking your time for two weeks, by the minute, to see exactly how you spend your days. Be sure to include everything you do, such as the amount of time you sleep and watch television, computer and phone time, and the time you spend with your family and friends. This will give you information that will enable you to use your available time more efficiently. It will also show you where you might be wasting time that could be put to better use.

If you are a detail person and you want to find every extra available minute in your day, take your planning to another level by choosing to use a daily planner sheet that is formatted by the quarter hour.

When you work from home, interruptions and distractions are un-avoidable. With strategic planning, there are ways that you can minimize the distractions or even keep them from happening completely.

Having a clear business vision, complete with the necessary projects listed to achieve it, will keep you more focused and time-conscious and will make your daily planning time even more valuable. Find information for preparing your business plan in Sheri Cockrell's chapter, *Business Planning for the Serious Mom Entrepreneur*, on page 57.

Based on your business vision, determine the specific projects that will be required to achieve your goal. Once you have them listed, verify the objective of each project, break it down into necessary tasks and then set a start date and deadline for each task. As you are planning, you may realize that you will require help with some of your projects. Who will you ask?

Create your "absolutely needs to be done" list. To maximize the use of your time, use your projects and tasks list to create a daily "absolutely needs to be done" list. These are the essential projects and tasks that need to be done that day. On your daily time sheet or in your planner, block off the specific time you will do each task.

Once you have your list and time blocked off to complete those items, you will be able to distinguish any open time blocks you have available for other tasks you would like to include.

When you are creating your list, always choose the things you know will have the biggest impact on your day. Check your list against your business plan and your family priorities. Do they match? Is everything listed in agreement with your priorities and business goals?

Utilize time blocking for all aspects of your business. The first things to include in your planner would be the blocks of time for any constants that you have in your life. These are the things that happen every day, week or month—at the same time every day, week or month.

Some examples of constants would be:

• children's sports activities

• daily, weekly and monthly planning time

• scheduled phone calls or training for your business

• any personal appointments like getting a manicure

Having them included will remove the possibility of scheduling an appointment over already-scheduled family or business commitments.

In addition to constants, projects, tasks and appointments, schedule time to take care of ordinary email correspondence, phone calls and social networking. Not doing this makes them a huge distraction and a possible time-waster.

Use a timer. The use of an ordinary kitchen timer can easily add meaningful minutes to your day. Set the timer for the amount of time you have blocked off for a task. Using the timer will cancel the need to watch the clock and you can stay laser-focused and amplify the impact you have on the task at hand. This can also significantly increase your productivity as you focus your efforts to beat the clock.

Delegate. This will enable you to stay on target and address the projects and tasks that matter most and that will enable you to attain your goals faster. Realize that you don't have to do everything yourself. Delegating tasks and projects will free up valuable time that you can use for projects that need your personal attention.

When you create your daily "absolutely needs to get done" list, highlight the tasks that you absolutely need to do and check the ones that you can delegate to others. One way to determine if a task is something that should be delegated is to ask yourself this question: "Based on my business vision and my expectations, is this the best use of my time?"

Purchase a hand-held tape or digital recorder and keep it available at all times. How many times have you had a great idea and before you were able to get it on paper, you forgot it? Using a recorder is definitely much safer than searching for a pen and paper when your epiphany arrives as you are driving down the highway! No more searching for little scraps of paper. A tape recorder or using the recording application on your smartphone will save time—and your sanity. Transcribing the recording could be something that you choose to delegate.

Keep multitasking to a minimum. Contrary to popular belief, multitasking really is not the best way to conduct your business. Being laser-focused on a task will not only ensure that it is done correctly and to the best of your ability, it actually makes it possible to accelerate the completion of the task.

As with all rules, there can be exceptions. Here are a few ways to turn multitasking into time expanders while you are waiting for an appointment or for your children to be ready to be picked up.

Have a resource box in your car. Make sure it contains:

- A book that you have on your "want to read" list

- A small notebook entitled "Ideas for Business Growth" which you can use for inspiration and brainstorming to create new projects that will move your business forward and add revenue to your bottom line

- Articles from magazines that pertain to your business

- Training or inspirational CDs and MP3s

- Note cards for catching up on correspondence

With all of the portable electronics available, this is also the perfect time to catch up on texts, emails and phone calls.

Stop procrastinating. Everyone occasionally procrastinates. The task you are avoiding won't get any easier or more enjoyable. Putting the task off could result in stress or a sense of guilt or could keep you from being your best and achieving your business goals. Make it a habit to take out your planner, block off time to get it done, do it and then celebrate your success. Remember, you can always delegate.

Learn to say no. The best way to expand your time is to learn to say no to people and opportunities that are not in line with your business vision, values and priorities. Saying no will instantly give you more available time in your day. The time it adds can be used to accelerate the achievement of your business goals, produce stellar products and services and allow you to spend more time with your family.

Saying no is not an easy thing to do. However, as one of my coaching clients discovered, it is well worthwhile. She began to focus on why, how and when to say no based on her family and business priorities, which leveraged and maximized her time.

Here are some examples of saying no politely.

- *In all fairness to you, I can't say yes. I know I don't have the time to give it the proper attention it deserves.*

- *I have so many commitments to others. It would be unfair to them and you if I took on another commitment at this time.*

- *Your project deserves someone who can really be focused and would have the time to make it a priority. I just can't be that person.*

- *I know you'll understand when I have to say no. Just like you, sometimes I find myself completely over-scheduled and this is one of those times.*

You may also need to say no to watching too much television, spending too much time on social media or attending meetings and events that are not in line with your business vision.

Get and stay organized. In addition to being organized with planning your time, it is a good practice to be organized with your workspace. When everything has a place and is in its place, you are better prepared to work more effectively. An organized space will also expand your productivity as it eliminates clutter and makes it possible for you to quickly locate what you need without having to sort through papers or files.

Being organized on your computer is as important as having an organized office space. Develop a system for naming, storing and saving files on your computer that is simple and easy to remember.

Being able to quickly locate the information you need will save you hours of time and frustration.

Schedule time for you. The savvy mom entrepreneur has figured out the perfect blend for her family and business. She is organized, and she knows that with all work and no play there is a good chance that the rest of her family will not be happy.

As you are planning for the successful blending of family and career, be consistent in scheduling time in your planner for you. The most successful work-from-home moms realize they are responsible for keeping themselves energized, renewed and at their best. Taking breaks to pamper yourself will help extinguish burnout and will facilitate exceptional results for your business, garnering enthusiasm and support from your family.

Review your day. In addition to taking a moment to enjoy the best things that happened, reflecting on the day's events will give you a keener perspective of what worked and what didn't. It will generate inspiration and information for new projects, spark ideas for improving what you are currently doing, guide you to finding ways to do things more efficiently or differently, and clarify what you need to do more of or not at all. It can also be your barometer for deciding on your future answers of yes or no.

Being the best mom entrepreneur doesn't mean that you have to be superwoman or supermom. It just means that you need to know what your family believes are the most important things you do for them and make sure you include them in your daily planning.

There's nothing more rewarding as a mom than to be there for your family through all the stages of their lives. Living life as a mom entrepreneur makes it possible to have the best of both worlds.

Martha Staley, CDC

Your Perfect World®
– Direct Selling Success Strategies
Your Perfect Day. . . your way. . . every day!
(618) 569-5655
martha@yourperfectworld.net
www.directsellingsuccessstrategies.com
www.yourperfectworld.net

Martha Staley is the founder and CEO of Your Perfect World, a direct sales trainer and speaker, and Certified Dream Coach®. Her passion is empowering women to live the life of their dreams every day, not just some days. She believes that you have the power to create and live in your own unique world based on your personal values, priorities and the realities of your ever-changing life and circumstances.

As a mom and a direct sales professional for over 20 years, Martha understands the daily challenges mom entrepreneurs experience. The training Martha provides for companies, individuals and organizations through her speaking, coaching, teleclasses and workshops generates positive results. Her programs, based on proven strategies and systems she created and used to grow her own multi-million dollar organization, improve her clients' ability to achieve their business results more quickly than they expect.

She is a co-author of the book *Direct Selling Power*, published by PowerDynamics Publishing in 2010, a member of the Direct Selling Women's Alliance, a DSWA Certified Elite Leader, contributor to the DSWA's *Mentored by the Masters* program, and a member of the International Coach Federation and The National Association of Professional Women.

From Business Suit to Bathing Suit

Mastering Business Travel with Family and Kids
By Cindy Sakai, MAOM, CDC

"The secret of your success is making
your vocation your vacation."
—Mark Twain, American author and humorist

I am a wife, mom and business owner. When I started my company with my business partner, Sarah Kalicki-Nakamura, we did it with work-life balance in mind. I was single with no kids and Sarah was married with a baby boy. I knew that someday I would get married and start a family and I wanted to be a mom who would be around to create family memories while having a career at the same time. Entrepreneurship was the solution.

Sarah and I shared the vision of owning a successful business doing something we loved while making our families our main priorities. Out of this idea came a training and development company known today as TH!NK, LLC. Five years into our business, I relocated from Hawaii to California for my spouse's career and within a year had my son, Hudson. Motherhood changed my life, and motherhood with business travel turned my world upside down.

Business travel with my son started when he was three months old. Since then I have learned many lessons, and somehow business trips with Hudson allowed us to blend business and pleasure. This afforded great family vacations while I was still growing my business. Over the years I have found myself giving tips to traveling moms, from packing the suitcase to surviving the airplane, from managing time zones to what to do when the family stays home. In this chapter, I will share what I have learned about making my vocation my vacation and creating a win-win for the whole family.

To Take the Kids or Not? Factors to Consider

Deciding whether or not to take a business trip with your family is a tough one. Here are a few things to consider:

1. What are your non-negotiables? My first advice to any business mom is to know the things you will not negotiate and then schedule around those priorities. In this way, you will never deceive yourself nor regret your choices.

Non-negotiables for you might be:

- **School schedules:** When are the school vacation breaks? School performances? Parent-teacher conferences? Parent-volunteer days?

- **Financial budget:** Be clear about your budget for each trip you take. Anticipate the hidden costs of travel such as family meals, admissions into family venues and childcare.

- **Spouse's work schedule:** Communicate work schedules regularly. Every Sunday, my husband and I sit down with our calendars and get clear on the week's schedule. I also keep a virtual calendar, which he accesses for schedule updates.

- **Health-related issues:** Are there any illnesses or conditions that restrict how much you can travel?

- **Length of time away from family:** Know what your travel limits are. Is it your goal to be able to tuck the kids into bed every night? If so, you will be a short-distance traveler and home every evening. Do you want to be away from home no longer than three days? Maybe seven days is your limit. Determine what is okay with you, your family and your support system.

- **Any additional criteria** that are pertinent to your family and business.

Note: Let no one else define or judge what should be important to you and your family; *you* define it.

Once you know your non-negotiables, plot them on your calendar and identify the blocks of time that you *can* travel—with kids and without kids. For example, you may be limited to the school vacation schedule if you have school-aged children, or your business trips may be limited by how much childcare support you have. This immediately takes the guilt out of business travel because you have prioritized what is important and have a schedule that you control. In the end, your clients are better served because your travel availability is already mapped out.

2. What support do you have on the other end? If you travel with family on business, know who will provide support with childcare while you are away at a meeting or when you need work time while your children are awake. During my son's first two years of travel to Hawaii, my mother was available to babysit while I was working. She was either already in Hawaii or I would bring her with me on trips. As other priorities and health issues became a factor and she was not able to assist, I had to look at other resources. I called friends for babysitter referrals, traded babysitting favors and even considered treating friends to a trip in exchange for babysitting services.

3. Can you balance business goals and family? Be clear about your business trip goal and the length of the trip. Will your family benefit by being with you or will everyone be miserable? Do you have room in your schedule for playtime or is this a fast-paced business trip? If your business trip schedule ties you up more than 70 percent of your children's waking hours, you will have to consider whether or not a family business trip is a good idea and really look at how everyone can benefit.

4. Can you afford it? Know how you will fund the personal travel expenses of your family. Is your child young enough to fly for free? If you need to travel with a nanny or spouse, can you fly them on airline reward miles? Budget everything—accommodations, meals, excursions, and so on. If your business trips repeatedly take you to the same destination, invest in memberships such as the local zoo, museums or aquariums. Those dollars will save you money in the long run. Ideally, stay with family and friends if you are fortunate enough to have that option. Otherwise, select family-friendly hotels that provide full or partial kitchenettes, free meals such as complimentary breakfasts or kids-eat-free deals. You will also want to consider other hidden costs of travel, including the costs of not being at home. For example, for us, placing our dog in a kennel could cost the equivalent of airfare for one person. We opted instead for housesitters or dogsitters, which sliced our costs by 70 percent.

Packing Smart

How and what you pack in your suitcase can make or break you. Literally. You can become a pack mule getting to and from your destination. This is about your physical survival. Later, we will discuss your emotional survival. Right now, though, we are talking about you emerging pain-free after getting you, your child(ren) and the suitcases through all points of the travel process before reaching your destination. My friend refers to this as "troop movement" if you are traveling with more than three people in your party. If you are traveling with a small child, ask yourself these three questions:

1. How will I get to the check-in counter without leaving my child waiting on the curb?

2. How will I retrieve my luggage and get it to the curb without leaving my child waiting on the curb?

3. How will I get to the rental car bus in one fell swoop—again, without leaving my child on the curb?

Get the picture? How can you get through each travel phase while keeping your family safe? Once you get to your destination, you can relax a little more. Hotels have bellmen and family homes have free "bellmen."

Suitcase Strategy

As you can see from the above, a suitcase strategy is important. Ideally, the fewer the bags, the better. My rule of thumb is one suitcase per suitcase-carrying human. If you are traveling alone with your two-year-old, limit yourself to one suitcase. If you are traveling with two adults and two toddlers, limit your luggage to two suitcases. If you have a child who can manage his or her own suitcase, you are allowed another suitcase.

The Carry-on Choice

Your choice of carry-on is a big deal. I have tried every possible alternative for a carry-on that would allow me to carry laptop, diapers, baby bottles, sippy-cup, baby wipes, spare clothes, toys, and so on. Until your children can wheel their own mini-backpacks—my son started when he was three years old—limit yourself to one carry-on. If at all possible, use a bag that can be wheeled. After five years, and many stiff necks and backaches later, I have defined the features of my now ideal carry-on bag:

- In-line skate wheels—they glide for quickness and ease.

- Made of durable, lightweight, soft, washable material. Soft material allows the bag to squish under the seat and not have to go into the overhead bin. You'll have everything available to you when you need it.

- Thin enough to fit down the narrow airline aisles. This makes a huge difference. Many laptop briefcases cannot be wheeled easily down the aisle and you have to pick them up and carry them. This is tough to do if you have to help or carry kids down the aisle. My current favorite is the Brighton® weekender bag with dimensions of 19"W x 14"H x 7½"D.

- Large enough to carry a laptop and those baby or young toddler essentials. Remember the "one carry-on" rule.

- Ample pockets to keep you organized.

- Durable telescoping handle that won't bend or break when your child hops on your carry-on for a thrill ride.

Surviving the Airplane

The average duration of an airplane ride that I travel with my son is five hours, and we have successfully done up to fourteen hours getting from California to the Bahamas in one day without a meltdown. By the time I did the fourteen-hour flight, I already had three years of traveling with him six times a year. I am certain that what I knew by then led to a tantrum-free trip. The following strategies are designed to help you keep your mental sanity, help others sitting within earshot not want to strangle you, and support your child(ren) in having a good time.

Make it a new surprise. Most importantly, plan your children's plane activities and what you need to bring for them. Toys that feel new to them will capture their interest twice as long! Pack toys, books, coloring books and activities that are either new or that have not been seen or used in a long time. Ever notice how an old lost toy rediscovered captures attention like a new toy? Save the good stuff for the plane. Whenever I see clearance sales of toys that are quiet, travel-size, non-liquid, that I know my son would love and I know will not be confiscated at security, I stock up on them. The night before we leave, after he is asleep, I pack the carry-on and keep it sealed until we get past the security line or even better, until we get on the plane.

Toys to avoid. Avoid toys that will cause havoc on the plane.

• Anything that produces any sound but does not have a volume button or that cannot be hooked up to headphones.

• Toys and puzzles with little pieces—no Legos® or stringing beads. They easily get lost and some kids become obsessed with retrieving fallen pieces, ending up crawling under seats into neighboring passengers.

• Anything that rolls or bounces. Balls and marbles roll under seats and feet, traveling quickly during ascents and descents.

• Sticky toys. No Play-Doh®, Slime® or Moon Sand®. I have seen them on the plane — they make a mess and eventually become airborne!

Airplane tips for babies (pre-walking). The infant stage can sometimes be the easiest stage for travel because infants sleep more. Preparation is still key at this stage:

- Pack a 24-hour supply of baby food and milk. It is essential that you be ready for that nightmare delay at the airport.

- Research ahead of time which airlines are kid-friendly. For a while I only flew airlines that had baby-changing tables that dropped down over the bathroom toilet.

- The crawling stage can be challenging. Your infant wants to move, yet you are afraid of the germs they will pick up on their hands and body. Big tip! Bring an extra footy pajama that you can zip over their clothes. Then, put soft infant shoes, for example, Robbies®, on their hands and let them crawl on the floor if you have to. Once they are done, unzip everything and put it in a plastic bag to keep it separated from the clean clothes. This really helps to manage all that baby energy!

Board last. This goes against the conventional wisdom that travelers with young children need to board first. That's only if you are traveling with everything but the kitchen sink! If you are traveling with just one carry-on per adult, then you can do this, even if you are wheeling a stroller down the runway. This will only work if there are assigned seats on the plane. If you board last, you will be able to do the following:

- Expend more child-energy before being stuck on the plane.

- Possibly get better seats on the plane. I discovered that boarding late opens up the possibility of getting an empty row of seats. Ever notice that everyone is watching for the empty seats and just before take-off people are jumping to secure those roomier seats? If you board last, you get to grab those open seats first. Each time I did this, my son napped longer because he could fully lay out and sleep. I could get work done on my laptop because he was not partially sleeping on me. With the extra space, kids can get more creative playtime without interrupting others. My son's favorite activity is tucking the plane blankets into the headrest and service trays to make a tent. Flight attendants play along with him, peeking into his tent to chat with him and serve him snacks. It's a win for everyone.

- If the airlines are assigning standby seats after you have boarded, then you will have to use your charm to negotiate keeping your treasured extra seats.

- If you can, book flights on low-travel days to ensure more available seats on the plane.

Destination Reached — Now What?

You have arrived and unpacked, and now you are ready to work and play. Balancing the two can be tricky. Again, if you plan, your vocation becomes your vacation!

Managing work and play time. Schedule your work and play time and communicate it to those traveling with you. Aside from in-person business meetings and commitments, work while the family is sleeping, which means waking up early and buckling down once they go down. Communicate to your family daily what the plan is and stick to the plan. When work and play time are clearly delineated, they will ask less. When it is time to play, do it whole-heartedly. Send unimportant phone calls to voicemail, and let clients know when you are and are not available.

Stay healthy. Nothing is worse than sabotaging a vacation or business trip by getting sick. Pack your vitamins and take them! This is not the time to skimp on supplements, eating healthy or getting lots of rest. This also goes for everyone traveling with you.

Managing time zones. The first two days of being in a different time zone will affect sleep patterns. Build flexibility with light schedules into your first days, allowing for the time differences. When returning home, your productivity is affected by how everyone sleeps. I have found that for every week spent away, it takes one day to adjust back to normal sleep patterns. If you have been away for two weeks, it takes two days to get back to normal; three days for three weeks. Four days is the maximum if your trip is longer than four weeks.

When Family Stays at Home

Most of my business trips are to Hawaii, and when people hear that I am going alone, the room fills with "Ohhhhh" and they envision me on the beach with a mai tai in my hand. The benefits of solo business trips are obvious. You get more work done, tackle projects that require fierce, laser-like concentration and can squeeze in a pedicure at a moment's notice.

Leaving family at home requires as much preparation as taking them with you—with a twist. Here are some strategies to make it all work when you will be traveling alone.

- Start talking about your trip two weeks in advance so that children get used to the idea. You want them to be practically bored by the details of your trip so that when you leave, it is not a big deal.

- Communicate with your spouse or caregiver about schedules and prepare as much as possible before you leave. For example, wrap the birthday gift your child needs to take to Friday's birthday party, purchase the snack your child has to bring on her day to bring the class snack and so on.

- Prepare little surprises each day while you are away. Little messages or gifts, special snacks, music—anything that brings a smile to your little ones are quick reminders that Mom is thinking about them.

- Good morning, good night. Call the family at the start of each day and at the end of each day. Be one of the first and last voices they hear while you are away.

- Stay in touch via webcam if you have one.

- Keep the family busy with fun activities while you are away.

- Pre-plan a fun outing that everyone looks forward to upon your return.

- Schedule no work for one to two days after your return and just focus on family.

Last Thought —
Mom Entrepreneur to Mom Entrepreneur

Traveling on business with family is simply one of the best benefits of being a mom entrepreneur! While it is never perfect, with planning and creative thinking, anything is possible and you can practically have your cake and eat it too. Enjoy the process, don't sweat the small stuff, keep your eye on your priorities and relish the thought that you have turned your vocation into your vacation.

Cindy Sakai, MAOM, CDC

Training Resultant and co-owner
TH!NK, LLC

(808) 936-4992
cindy@think-training.com
www.think-training.com

Cindy Sakai is a wife, mother and entrepreneur who believes that we all have the power to create our best life. She is inspired by the entrepreneurial strength of her mother, Jeanette Taam, who created a thriving in-home tutoring business in order to be a stay-at-home-mother for three young daughters after losing their father to cancer.

As co-owner of TH!NK, LLC, a training and development company, Cindy is a training resultant and executive coach who helps leaders transform their people in order to maximize results. Recognized with the Emerald Award from Inscape Publishing and as a PBN Business Leadership 2010 finalist for Innovative Company of the Year, TH!NK, LLC serves organizations such as the United States Army, Oceanic Time Warner Cable®, Goodwill Industries of Hawaii® and McDonald's Restaurants® of Hawaii.

As a Certified Dream Coach®, trained Purposeful Coach and a DiSC® practitioner since 2000, Cindy has the gift of trans-forming leaders by uncovering their hidden potential. Cindy is also a co-author of *Direct Selling Power*, published in 2010 by PowerDynamics Publishing, where she shares her expertise on creating a business model that values relationships yielding high-end results.

136

Rediscovering Recess

Create a Game Plan for Adding More Fun to Your Life
By Jennifer Malocha, AAS, ACSM, NSCA

"It's fun to have fun but you have to know how!"
— Theodor S. Geisel ("Dr. Seuss"), American author and cartoonist

*H*ave you watched your children playing at recess? They are totally carefree! Do you remember what recess was like when you were in school? It was fun, filled with laughter, fellowship, movement and the ability to do anything *you* wanted.

Rediscovering recess is not child's play—it's acknowledging that as a mother, business owner and creative person, how essential it is to make time in life for play and self-care. By making time for what is important, you can better focus on reaching your goals, maintaining your highest level of energy and creativity and enjoying all that life has to offer.

Recess means taking a break from doing all those things that you *have* to do and making time to focus on all the things you *get* to do. How often do you take time to do special things you *know* will add joy and pleasure to your busy, full life?

In this chapter, I will help you see the importance of making time for yourself and show you how to create rules and a game plan which will give you the structure and the vitality to follow through with your plans on your journey to making your dreams a reality!

Think about the game you most enjoy playing. That game has rules to follow and a goal to strive for. As a mom entrepreneur, you create your own set of rules and your own goals.

In order to determine the rules for *your* game, you have to be clear about the game you are choosing to play. One aspect of the game I will teach you to play is about adding more fun to your life. In order to be both a wonderful mom and a successful entrepreneur you need balance, which is the ultimate goal of *this* game.

Sometimes you may feel as if you have no breathing room in your life. You have so much to do, there's no time left for anything enjoyable. You feel as if you have no choices. In reality, you *always* have choices about your life. After all, it is *your* life and you are in complete charge of *you*. Everyone has similar abilities expressed through different gifts, and we all have the same number of hours in a day to complete everything that needs to be done. The key is to make sure you include time for replenishing yourself daily, even if it's only a few minutes each day.

Time Out! Taking Time to Take Care of Yourself

Taking time for self-care is critical. As a mother, you are the caretaker. You take care of your kids, your house, your business, your friends, your parents, and so on. You may even volunteer for various organizations.

Often *you* end up at the bottom of the "take-care-of" list—if you make it onto the list at all. Not taking care of yourself is the most selfish thing you can do. That's right, I said "selfish."

When you take care of yourself you have more energy, are less stressed, enjoy better health and can be your best for everyone, especially those you love the most. When you don't take care of yourself, the opposite is true. You give the ones you love someone who is stressed out, short-tempered and frazzled. Everyone suffers.

Remember that you are a role model for your children daily. When you take care of yourself you teach your children that practicing good self-care is important. The girls will learn to make self-care a priority in their own lives. The boys, who already assume that they will take care of themselves, will learn that women, too, need to take care of themselves and they will expect and support that for the women in their lives. It is imperative that moms realize this so they can be the best role models possible for their children of either gender.

There are many creative ways of taking care of yourself that don't take a lot of time or money. I encourage you to get creative! Here is a list of ideas that will help get you started:

- Go for a walk, a bike ride or a swim.

- Meditate or attend church.

- Do yoga or simple stretching.

- Read a book just for fun.

- Pamper yourself and get a massage, a pedicure, a manicure, or a facial.

- Go to lunch or see a movie with a friend or by yourself!

- Take dance, craft or art classes or sign up to play on a sports team.

- Eat more vegetables and fruit.

- Take a nap.

- Work in your garden or just sit in it and enjoy the fruits of your labor.

- Sing in a choir.

*"Our lives are a mixture of different roles. Most of us are
doing the best we can to find whatever the right balance is . . .
For me, that balance is family, work and service."*
—Hillary Rodham Clinton, 67th United States Secretary of State

In order to show the importance of taking care of yourself from a fiscal perspective, here are some statistics that were compiled in 2007 by DeVol, et al., the Centers for Disease Control (CDC), PricewaterhouseCoopers, and Partnership to Fight Chronic Disease (PFCD).

The Cost of Health Care

- In 1987, adults spent $272 a year per person for health care.

- In 2001, adults spent $1,244 for the same health care.

- In 2007, the average cost of health insurance was $4,242 per person, $11,480 for a family of four.

- That's an increase of almost $4,000 a year in the last 20 years.

- More people are sick with conditions linked to obesity such as diabetes and high blood pressure than ever before.

- By 2023, there will be a 42 percent increase in costs from these diseases, which equals $4.2 *trillion* (DeVol, et al., 2007).

The Cause of the Rise in Health Care Costs

- Already there is a $1.3 trillion impact on the economy from seven chronic diseases: cancer, diabetes, hypertension, stroke, heart disease, and mental and pulmonary illness (DeVol et al., 2007).

- The world has more people who are overweight than are starving (PricewaterhouseCoopers 2007).

- Chronic illness is responsible for seven out of ten deaths in the United States (PFCD 2007).

- Sixty percent of adult Americans don't get the recommended amount of physical activity per day.

- Fifty percent of adult Americans have a poor diet (CDC 2007).

Obesity is caused by a serious lack of self-care. As self-employed mom entrepreneurs, we simply cannot afford to not take care of ourselves—the cost is just too great.

Rule #1: Create and Honor a Master Schedule

Even though balance is always your ultimate goal, it's challenging as a mom entrepreneur to create balance on a daily basis—or even on a weekly basis. However, if you look at the month as a whole unit, you can see certain patterns emerge, which is how you will discover what you are doing well and for what you need to make more time.

One way to help you find time in your schedule for self-care is to create a master schedule that includes self-care. Treat self-care appointments with the same priority as other appointments and make sure you honor these appointments.

I have found that color-coding my calendar using different colors for various commitments and activities in my life helps create more balance and breathing space. Breathing space is the groundwork for playtime. Choose a different color for every activity in your life. My color coding includes work time as dark green for money, business development as light green, family time as dark blue, spiritual time as light blue, date night as red and so on.

Before I implemented my master schedule I found myself thinking about my family during work time, which made me feel guilty about being away from them. I would think about my work during family time, which made me feel guilty about being away from work. I felt like I never had time to do the things I wanted to do outside of work and family. It was a vicious cycle! I ended up feeling like I never did anything right. When I finally created the master schedule, complete with color-coding, it made it easy to see where I was out of balance, which allowed me to make changes and create desperately needed breathing space. The result was a happier, more productive mom entrepreneur who had a much happier husband and kids.

Self-care guarantees that the ones you love the most get the best of you, which is the epitome of selflessness. Make time for yourself every day, even if it is only for a few minutes—your family deserves it and so do you!

Rule #2: Define Your Strategy and Navigate the Obstacles

Once you create your master schedule, you can brainstorm potential obstacles that might get in the way. This helps you create strategies for working around them in order to achieve your goal of finding balance.

When you are prepared it does not matter what may come up. You will not be thrown off course, or worse, stopped in your tracks, since you have options for achieving your goal. For example, what will you do if your child is sick or if your husband has to travel at the last minute? Maybe you can arrange with a friend or family member to do emergency childcare and then return the favor. Get creative with finding solutions to obstacles that come up.

It is perfectly normal if your timeline changes or even if your goals change. After all, life is unpredictable and ever-changing. The important thing is to keep moving forward.

Rule #3: Set Personal Boundaries

Being clear on your personal boundaries is an important step in the process of creating fun and finding joy in your life. It is up to you to decide who you let into your life and who you do not let in, and— most importantly—how you want people to treat you. If you do not like how someone treats you, or you feel he or she is not supportive, it is up to you to set your own personal boundaries with that person.

Remember, you are in control; you have the power to determine how you are treated and who you want in your life. Establishing and honoring your personal boundaries is crucial in making sure the people in your life treat you with kindness, love and respect. Of course, the most important person in your life who needs to treat you with kindness, love and respect is you.

The first step in creating boundaries is to pay attention to how you feel during and after interactions with certain people. Do you feel uplifted and energetic or do you feel tired and drained? If you feel tired and drained, then it is important to limit your interactions with that particular person or group of people whenever possible. The next step, which is not always easy, is to say no when you want to say no. When you say yes to something that you do not want to do, you often end up resenting the task as well as the person who asked you to perform the task. By asking for 24 hours to decide, you have just created breathing space. Be very clear how you contribute to how people treat you. If you do not like how you are treated, it is up to you to make the necessary changes that will result in people treating you in the way you wish to be treated from this point forward.

Rule #4: Create a Support Team to Pull You through Tough Times

"Nobody can do everything, but everyone can do something."
—Author Unknown

Relying on others to create the balance you desire is critical. Regardless of how amazing you are, you cannot do everything by yourself—at least not well. Something has to give, and it is usually you.

Create your very own support team. These are the people who will give you a hug, a pat on the back or a kick in the pants when you need it. They will offer invaluable insights, help you problem-solve, become strategic alliance partners and be fantastic resources for achieving the goal of balance in your life.

I volunteer as a "swim angel" for the Seattle Danskin Triathlon®. My task is to swim the course with a swim noodle in tow looking for women in the middle of the course who, for some reason, seem to have forgotten how to swim. I come up to them and say, "Hi! My name is Jennifer, what's yours? Isn't it a beautiful day?" Once I get their attention, I offer them the noodle to rest on and get them talking to me. I help them remember that they know how to swim, get them to take a few deep breaths, gather their resources, and assess the situation so that they can continue on their journey.

How often have you started out strong on a goal only to get halfway there and realize you have forgotten your way, or why you're doing it in the first place? You say to yourself, "Well, it *seemed* like a good idea at the time. What was I thinking?" Like the swimmers, you seem to forget how to swim. You forget how strong you are, how capable you are and what a really good idea it *is*. At times like this, you need someone on your support team to remind you that you really *do* know how to swim and that your goal is a noble one. You are just a bit scared. It is okay to be scared as long as you do not let that fear steal your dreams and goals.

The swim course, like life, is filled with people who are ready to jump in and help you. These people cheer you on, offer guidance and give you support when you need it most. I ask my swimmers to pick a target to swim to. By doing this, I help them focus on the next step. When they look at the whole swim course, it's too big and daunting. When they break it down, the goal becomes manageable. Your support team members are the swim angels for your life. They will help you see the next step along the route to achieving your goals.

Most women I know are the first ones to cheer someone on or lend a helping hand, yet these same women are the last ones to ask for help or to talk about their successes. Think about a time when you were asked for help. Did you give it? Of course you did! How good did it make you feel to be of service? When you ask for help, you give someone else the chance to have the warm, fuzzy feeling that comes from being of service. That is all part of being on a team.

Make Your Balanced Life a Reality

As a mom entrepreneur, I have learned through experience the importance of the rules I have outlined in this chapter for rediscovering recess in my own life. When you know what is most important to you and take the time to care for yourself and follow a plan, you reduce the stress in your life—allowing yourself to enjoy each area of your life more fully. When you take time for yourself, you are able to focus on the next step, which creates breathing space on your journey toward achieving your goals.

A life that is all work and no play seems pretty bleak. On the other hand, a life that is balanced with love, laughter and prosperity is the definition of a dream life. Go ahead and start rediscovering recess in your own life today. You will be glad you did and so will everyone else around you.

Jennifer Malocha,
AAS, ACSM, NSCA

Wuhoo Fitness

(206) 601-2485
jennifer@wuhoofitness.com
www.wuhoofitness.com

Jennifer Malocha takes the business of having fun very seriously. With a wellness coaching certification, six different fitness certifications and a degree in fitness, she's at the top of her game. As her clients reap the benefits of all that training, they start to figure out her secret— she's having a ball too! Running, walking, swimming—Jennifer loves it all and her enthusiasm spills into everything she does.

Life hasn't always been so much fun. She's overcome childhood abuse, lost a beloved brother and conquered teenage addiction. She acknowledges her involvement in sports for helping her get through many tough spots. Jennifer has gone through a lot to get where she is today, and now she wants to play!

With a thriving fitness and coaching business as well as a track record studded with accomplishments—Jennifer has coached over 150 women across the finish line of their first triathlon—she helps people make changes that affect every aspect of their lives. Knowing that small changes over time yield huge results, Jennifer's passion is bringing joy to others through fitness and play.

Authentically You

Making Your Mom Entrepreneur Life Work
Using the Law of Attraction
By Tania Boutin, CLC, NLSC, SDC

"Personal transformation can and does have global effects.
As we go, so goes the world, for the world is us. The revolution that
will save the world is ultimately a personal one."
—Marianne Williamson, American spiritual teacher and author

*I*nner transformation is one of those things that is ultimately left up to us. Becoming who we really want to be and finding our inner being cannot be accomplished by anyone else, yet it is one of the last things we look at when we want change in our lives. Why is that? It takes a lot of courage to push past the fear of looking and seeing what defines us. We usually just sit back and say that we do not have the time in our busy schedules to see what our identity is. However, we all want change in some part of our lives.

Being a mom entrepreneur is a juggling act. There is a heavy burden placed on our shoulders, trying to be the best mom that we can be while holding our business and household to high standards. Very seldom do we ask ourselves, "Who am I and what do I want from life?" If you sit back right now and ask yourself those questions, there will be many of you who will have no idea how to answer them. When I ask you to self-reflect, I'm not asking for your role as mother, daughter, sister or wife. I mean, who are you above and beyond those roles? How sad would it be to go through life and not know the meaning or purpose of what truly fulfills your soul? You have the power to create your future and discover your authenticity.

The mind is a powerful instrument that you have with you day after day. It structures your belief system. Beliefs are habits performed over and over again, proving to you that your thoughts are true. What happens if someone offers you another perception? Are you open to it? Remember that others' beliefs are their own habits that they have done consistently, which makes them right as well.

Your thoughts become your reality, and having positive thoughts—or turning a negative thought into a positive one—can have a tremendous effect on your life. Now, I do not mean simply ignoring or being in denial regarding any negative situations that are happening your life. What I am talking about is not letting your circumstances control you or your happiness. As stated in Marci Shimoff's book, *Happy For No Reason*, published by Free Press in 2008, your life situations only constitute 10 percent of your happiness. Forty percent represents your habits and the other fifty percent is genetics. Lucky for you, you can alter your genetics by your type of thinking, giving you ninety percent control of your thoughts! With this realization, you can see that you *do* have a hold over your mindset and the outcome. Just take that first step on your path to a life full of contentment and happiness.

Let's go over some tools to reach unconditional happiness, followed by discussing how to implement the law of attraction into your life to bring you continued accomplishment.

Attitude

Are you an optimist or pessimist? Is the glass half empty or half full? Your attitude determines your mindset, which is half the battle.

Choosing a positive attitude can make even the darkest situation have some light at the end of the tunnel. Knowing that there is a solution and looking for a way to solve it, instead of staying in that negative "victim" position, will change your whole outcome. Come from a position of knowing that you are powerful beyond measure with complete control.

Gratitude

When we appreciate all the good that we have in our life and pay attention to the details of what makes our life great, an abundance of happiness flourishes within and around us. A lot of the time it's the little things in life that we come to value. Saying "thank you" can make a big difference. Waking up in the morning and just being grateful can give you the start of a terrific day. Feel it in your heart when you are grateful for all you have in your life, even if it's just being alive! One good tool to use is a gratitude journal. At the end of the day, sit down with your journal and write down everything that made you smile that day. What were you thankful for? Do this every day, and when you take a look back, you will see just how much you have in your life.

> *"You become the average of the five people you associate with most."*
> — Jim Rohn, American entrepreneur, author and motivational speaker

Keeping Good Company

Surrounding yourself with the people who elevate and raise you up to be the best you can be will prove to be a stress reliever in and of itself. Being around people who are constantly demeaning and talking negatively can almost instantaneously lower your happiness level. By steering clear of those negative folks, and not letting their perceptions get in your way, you are going in the right direction. Emotions are very contagious and can influence you. Don't you think it would be great to grab hold of an uplifting feeling instead of anger, jealousy or anxiety? Your relationships, and the emotional energy surrounding them, can either build you up or tear you down. When viewing another person, acknowledge something that you appreciate about them. Instead of looking at what bothers you or what your different perceptions are, look at their unique and good qualities and what they have to offer. Appreciation will keep your happiness level high and will raise theirs as well.

Listen to Your Inner Voice

What is your self-talk saying to you? Is it positive or negative? Do you listen to those inner inklings when something bad is going to happen? Really taking the time to listen to what you are saying to yourself can help guide you to the many answers you have been looking for.

In the book, *Happy for No Reason,* the exercise entitled "Inner Listening" is one of Marci's many wonderful exercises that I love to do. It starts by asking you to take the time today to sit quietly with a paper and pen, write down what you want to know, then close your eyes, breathe deeply and ask your inner voice your question. Take the time to really listen, then when you are ready, open your eyes, start writing and keep writing whether it makes sense or not. Do not read as you go. Keep writing until your hand feels like it can no longer write anymore. When you are done, sit back and read. Even a single word or phrase can be the key to what you are looking for.

The comments you make to yourself have a lot of power. They control your life and your conclusions. The mind can make or break you, so be careful what you say to yourself.

Follow Your Passion

What is it that ignites your fire? What gets you so excited that you cannot wait until you can do it again? Finding your purpose doesn't just include your job—it is greater than that. What is your meaning in life? For instance, my passion is inspiring others to transform their lives to make them more fulfilling, happy and full of meaning and authenticity. Find out what it is that brings you joy and meaning. Ask yourself, "What would I choose if nothing could stop me from being and doing anything I want? What are my dreams?"

Law of Attraction

You are probably wondering how all of this applies to the law of attraction in transforming your life. We will now explore what the law of attraction is and how to apply it to your daily living and business.

Here are some points from leaders in the field of The Law of Attraction:

• "I attract into my life whatever I give my attention, energy and focus to, whether positive or negative." —Michael Loiser, Law of Attraction expert

• "That which is like unto itself is drawn."—Jerry and Esther Hicks, authors of *Ask and It Is Given*, published by Hay House in 2005

• "You are a living magnet; you attract into your life people, situations and circumstances that are in harmony with your dominant thoughts. Whatever you dwell on in the conscious, grows into your experience."—Brian Tracy, best-selling author and professional speaker

Law of attraction can also be described as something "out of the blue," "coincidental" or "karmic." Take a look at what is going on in your life from the outside and you will see what has been happening on the inside. The best news about this is, now that you know, you can do something about it! It is working whether you believe it or not. Why not make the most of it? You are probably thinking, why would I purposely attract anything negative into my life? The answer to that is, you don't—not consciously, but subconsciously through your thinking.

Can you see how this all ties in with your mindset and beliefs? When you are constantly thinking about something negative related to your business—for example, "this is such a struggle, I can never get anything accomplished"—you are programming your mind to believe that it is true. By taking the time to choose positive thoughts and encouraging yourself, you are setting yourself up for success.

This works through your vibration. A vibration is a mood or feeling you pick up from someone or something. It's either positive or negative. Have you ever walked into a room and felt either good or bad energy? Or have you met someone in whose presence you felt either good or bad? That is what your vibration is. The law of attraction is based on feelings or sensations. The way that you feel about yourself or a particular situation sends out a distinct vibration. Even if you say something positive to yourself, it could have no effect at all since it's all based on the way you feel about what you're saying. When you feel the passion, love and belief in what you are saying, you are sending out a positive vibration.

Your words are important. They turn into your thoughts, which then transform into your feelings of either positive or negative vibrations. Napoleon Hill, author of *Think and Grow Rich*, published most recently by CreateSpace in 2010, said it well: "Positive and negative emotions cannot occupy the mind at the same time. One or the other must dominate. It is your responsibility to make sure that positive emotions constitute the dominating influence of your mind."

When applying the law of attraction to your life and your business, there is a three-step process.

Step One

The first question you need to ask yourself is, "What do I want?" Identify what it is that you want in your life and your business and what you do not want. This is what is known as "contrast." By knowing what you do not want, it's easier to decipher what it is that you truly want in your presence, giving you clarity. The best way I have found to do this is by completing an exercise called "The Contrast to Clarity List," described by Michael Losier in his book, *Law of Attraction*, published by Wellness Central in 2010.

On a piece of paper, write at the top what it is that you wish to clarify. For example, you may write, "My Ideal Business." You then place a line down the middle of the page from the top. On the left hand side, write "Don't Want" and on the right side, write "Do Want." Now write what it is that you don't want, listing at least 50 things. Take your time. When that is complete, write all of the things you do want on the right side while crossing off the "Don't Wants" as you go along. Make sure you take that extra step to cross out the "Don't Wants." By crossing them off, it is like letting them go, which is very important. For example, if you wish a full client list within three months, you can put "struggling to get clients" on the left-hand side and write out on the righthand side, "Clients are easily attracted to me and I have a full practice within three months." Now cross off the "struggling to get clients" on the left-hand side.

Step Two

Now that you have identified what it is that you do want, give your desire attention—your positive energy and focus. Given that the law of attraction brings you more of what you give your energy, attention and focus to, you can understand why you want to give this desire all of your positive attention.

A good way of giving your desire the focus it needs is by using affirmations. An affirmation is a declaration spoken in the present tense and used to state a desire. For example, saying to yourself, "I have a successful business and clients are easily attracted to me" is an affirmation. Remember that the law of attraction responds to your feelings about the words you use and that a positive affirmation can still send out a negative vibration. Be conscious of bringing out positive feelings as you state your affirmations. If you are having trouble believing the words you are saying, rephrase the affirmation with "I am in the process of _____." That will make it more believable to you. It can be used for anything you wish to improve. For example, "I am in the process of becoming more abundant, growing my business and creating my ideal relationships." Anything you choose can be put into an affirmation. Make a list of at least 10 affirmations. Post them all over your home and read them daily.

Step Three
The last step in this process is to let it be. Allow it to happen. Sit back, relax and keep your positive focus on the desire. This is the hardest, yet most important, step because we think that if we let it be, nothing will happen. By mastering this step of allowing, you will be well on your way to attracting the business and life you desire.

There are some things you can do to have more "allowing" in your life. For starters, practice gratitude and appreciation as we discussed earlier. Take note of all the great parts of your life. This not only helps with your happiness level, it helps you attract a wonderful life. Another tool would be to have a vision board, book or box. Make a collection of all that you want in your life and business, from happiness to health, business expansion to more clients. Include everything internally and externally. Look at the board daily to keep your positive focus and say "thank you" for already having all of your desires happen. Put yourself in that feeling as already having it all. When you are getting on a call with a prospective client, hold the thought that you are attracting all of the clients who are best suited for you. When you get off the call, say "thank you" and be grateful for either a new client or the experience and opportunity to see that this client was not a match for you. You can have one vision board for your life in general and a separate vision board for business where you put all of your business goals.

Transforming your life and your business starts and ends with you. You have been given some tools to help you along your path to your true identity. Change is a challenge and can feel risky, and it's a risk worth taking. Pushing past your fear of knowing the inner you and expressing the total joy that you will have in your life reflects more than your inner and outer being. It also benefits your business and your relationships. By pushing past your comfort zone to reach within and find the authentic you, you are climbing up the transformation ladder and living a happy, fulfilling, purposeful life as a mom entrepreneur.

Knowing that you are your own person as well as a mom and business owner—and taking the time to discover who you really are and what you want—benefits your family as well as you. Being authentic and true to your needs, wants and values also teaches your family, friends and associates how to treat you. Put yourself in the right frame of mind and don't lose sight of your dreams. Climb high and reach for those stars!

Tania Boutin,
CLC, NLSC, SDC
**Transformational Coaching
with Tania**

Inspiring you to go from Ordinary to Extraordinary!

reclaimyourlife@taniaboutin.com
www.taniaboutin.com

Tania is a Certified Life Transformation Coach who loves to inspire women and mom entrepreneurs to live the authentic, happy life they deserve—guilt free! She does this by assisting them in the discovery of who they really are above and beyond the roles they play as mother, daughter, sister and wife, and showing them how to transform their life story into what they are longing for it to be.

Tania was raised in Iroquois Falls, Ontario, Canada. The environment in which she grew up helped foster her growth in many ways. Coming from a family of entrepreneurs, she learned early on the values of hard work and dedication. Hours spent in solitary introspection led to much spiritual and emotional growth.

After becoming a Certified Life Coach from CANA, Inc., she decided to continue in this field, specializing as a New Life Story Coach™ with Dr. David Kreuger of the Coach Training Alliance and as a Self-Discovery Coach™ through Merna Throne of the Self Discovery Coach Training Academy. Tania has joined forces with Compass as a representative and coach to offer affordable life coaching to all women!

Achieve Your Dreams Through Persistence

Know What You Really Want and How to Get It
By Karen Tucker, CDC

*D*o you find yourself wishing for a dream-come-true life, and doubting you can have it? Are you settling for what you have and where you are, yet longing for more? Is this what you want for the rest of your life? You can have anything if you are persistent enough to go after it. It's time to stop doubting and it's time to start taking action! You *can* have your dream-come-true life. It starts with you truly believing in who you are and getting clear on what you want.

Believing in Who You Are

If I were to ask you the question, "Who are you?"—how would you answer it? You would likely begin with answers like, "I am a woman, a mother, a wife, an entrepreneur, a member of my community," and so on. These are important aspects of who you are and yet you are more than what you do in life. Who are you at a core level? What is your essence? What contributions do you make just by being who you are? Is your nature tenderhearted and caring? Is it adventurous and outgoing? How are you unique? Can you truly believe in who you are and honor and cherish all of those things about you? I encourage you to do whatever it takes to step into the fullness of who you are and celebrate you!

Getting Clear on What You Want

If I were to ask you, "How would your life be if you could have it any way you want?"—what would you answer? The answer to this question is a crucial step in bringing clarity and direction to your life. It is a very important first step. Here are some tools that can assist you in making your vision real:

1. Imagine yourself already where you want to be. Imagine everything about it. Who are you with and what are you doing? What do you see, hear, smell? How do you feel inside? Paint the whole picture in your mind and settle into that vision.

2. Create a physical reminder of the life you want, either by drawing it, creating a collage around it or even simply writing it down. Put this reminder where you can see it all the time—on your mirror, your computer or your car visor, or in your planner.

3. Each day, each week and each month, set an intention to achieve what you want. Say it out loud or even share it with a friend or family member. Put a stake in the ground and make it happen.

4. Create a strategy and a plan to get what you want. Go after your dreams with every fiber in your soul. Make it real. Make it happen.

> *"It never occurred to me that I couldn't do it.*
> *I always knew that if I worked hard enough, I could."*
> —Mary Kay Ash, American entrepreneur
> and founder of Mary Kay, Inc.

Commit to Your Dream

Once you are clear about your dream, all it takes is commitment on your part to make it happen. Be someone you can be proud of. Be a role model for your children, family and others around you. People learn from what they see others do. Set the example and take the necessary steps. Delete the word "can't" from your vocabulary.

Only you are responsible for your success. Others can inspire you and give you hope, and *you* are the one who decides every day what you will accomplish to bring you closer to your dreams. You can do it if you want it badly enough and believe you can have it.

Develop the habits you need to move forward in accomplishing your dreams. Take responsibility for your life. When you do, everything will change. Begin today to create your dream-come-true life. What actions are you willing to take to demonstrate your commitment? Here are some steps to take:

Set goals. This is the single most important step you can take. After you get clarity on what it is that you want, begin setting goals for yourself. What will you do today that will move you toward your dream? What will you do this week? What is your goal for this month and next month? Create your goals and stick with them.

Educate yourself. To create the future you want, you must learn what you need to know in order to achieve your dream-come-true life. You need to discover and develop the talents that are within you. It doesn't matter where you are from, what education level you've reached, or how old you are. If you are persistent, you can learn what you need to know to achieve your dreams. Invest in yourself.

• Work with a coach to help you advance from one level to the next.

• Read and listen to resources that help you develop your self-worth.

• Join your local library so you have access to free books and books on tape or CDs.

• Attend seminars, conventions and events to meet people from whom you can gain knowledge.

Don't forget to use online resources to develop and grow. There are many free resources available for you to access online. Here are a few to try:

• www.skilledradio.com

• www.lesbrown.com

• www.dreamuniversity.com

Do you want to control your destiny? Now is the time to take action.

"Every great dream begins with a dreamer. Always remember you have within you the strength, the patience and the passion to reach for the stars to change the world."
—Harriet Tubman, African-American abolitionist and humanitarian

Encourage Others to Dream

While you are reaching for your own stars, encourage others to reach for theirs as well. Inspire each other along the way. I had the experience of others encouraging me and it made a huge difference in my life and profession.

In 1994, Avon®, the company for which I work, had a recruiting incentive. Within a five-month period, the top 50 recruiters in the United States would win trips to San Francisco. My intention was to win that trip. I recruited every day with great passion and sure enough, I won that trip. I was a little nervous about flying because I had never flown before. Living in the South, we didn't leave the nest very often, much less fly across the country by ourselves. However, I made the decision that I was going.

When I finally arrived in San Francisco, I was thrilled! At the reception dinner that first night, I met two "Valley Girls" from Los Angeles who were a lot of fun and made me feel welcomed and at home. They asked me if I had ever won any Avon trips before. I informed them that this was all new to me. They encouraged me to go after Avon's President Council trips where you had to sell $100,000 in a given year to win. They said that the best way to win the trip would be to help a club, group or organization raise money through an Avon fundraiser.

I made the decision right then and there that I was going to win the President Council trip that year, which was to Hawaii. By Christmas of 1994, my personal sales were $50,000. I needed to double that and I was determined to do it. My intention was set! I put a firm stake in the ground and took action. Here is what I did:

1. I contacted the local travel agent, got a poster of Hawaii, came home and posted it on the wall of my office where I looked at it every day.

2. I made a plan to do one big fundraiser plus at least ten small ones, and proceeded to take the necessary actions.

I wasn't stopping until I achieved what I needed. All of this was before computers were really "in," so I did it all by hand and on a calculator.

Within a few months time, I generated that additional $50,000 in sales and I did win that trip to Hawaii! That was the start of going on a yearly trip that I earned for each of the next 15 years.

"We can do anything we want to if we stick to it long enough."
—Helen Keller, American author, political activist and lecturer

Surviving Hurricane Katrina Helped Me

When Hurricane Katrina devastated my hometown of New Orleans on August 29, 2005, I sat in a hotel room watching the tragic news and knowing that half of my Avon representatives were losing their homes. I was devastated. We were told that we would be unable to go home for three to six months. My husband went home because of his job. My daughter and I headed to Florida. One month after I was there, my husband became ill and I knew my place was home, no matter what the conditions.

When I arrived home, it was a painful experience. I knew that I had to rebuild my business, repair the extensive damage to my home and be strong for my family. Immediately, I noticed that there were only a few stores open and I started to see an opportunity for sales. I also knew that in order to rebuild my downline and to help other representatives in my area who were finally making it back home, I had to be the leader God planned for me to be. I had to set the example so that others would follow.

Over the next three months I went out every weekend and set up tables of Avon products on the side of the road. Many people had still not returned to their homes. I had lost half of my team. It was very hard to find them because all of the phone lines, including cell phones, were out. Nevertheless, I was determined. I had to be the hope for the future. I had to have a way to reach others and show them how to get back to business, no matter what. I wanted to show them that it was okay to dream, even now—especially now—and that we would be okay. I will tell you it was not easy. It was a struggle and challenge every day, yet I persevered with deep conviction. Soon other Avon representatives began to emulate me.

I ended that year with an increase of over $100,000 in personal sales. The gift that this brought me was not only that I helped my family during a crisis and empowered many other women to not give up. I also earned the Avon Women of Enterprise Award for 2006. This was a huge dream-come-true for me. I was hoping to win this award at some point in my career, perhaps in ten years or so. However, this award came to me much sooner than I imagined. This award is quite prestigious—it gives you national recognition. You are flown in to speak at the national convention, and you have a special luncheon in your honor every year. I won this amazing, priceless award from among three million representatives, and it was because of the tragedy I went through and how I dealt with that adversity.

What I want you to learn from this experience is, no matter what you have to go through, you have to keep moving forward. Take the time to grieve, and know that you have what it takes to pull yourself through anything, that there is always a light on the other side, perhaps brighter than you could ever imagine.

You can read more about persevering through crisis in Tara Kennedy-Kline's chapter, *The Gifts in Being a Mom Entrepreneur,* on page 35.

The Only Special Skill You Need Is Persistence

Famous psychiatrist Dr. Joyce Brothers said, "Studies indicate that the one quality all successful people have is persistence. They are willing to spend more time accomplishing a task and to persevere in the face of many difficult odds. There's a very positive relationship between people's ability to accomplish any task and the time they're willing to spend on it."

Persistence means never giving up, always fighting a good fight and continuously marching forward. Be determined. Don't allow circumstances to run your life, learn how to run it yourself. The possibilities are endless. Believe in yourself. Take action. Be willing to pay the price. Know what you want in life and go after it with everything you have. Know why you are here; know your purpose. If I can do this, so can you.

Karen Tucker, CDC

Avon Independent Sales Representative and Senior Executive
(504) 628-5176
(866) 685-2866
karen@howtobepersistent.com
www.youravon.com/ktucker
www.howtobepersistent.com

Karen lives outside of New Orleans in the small town of Belle Chasse, Louisiana. She has been a stay-at-home, entrepreneurial mom since 1980 and knows how to get what she wants through the practice of persistence. Even after overcoming tragedy, Karen is a living example of never giving up.

After Hurricane Katrina, she bounced back by having a $100,000 Personal Sales Increase in her direct sales business and earned Avon's Women Of Enterprise Award in 2006. She holds the title of Senior Executive with Avon Products® and has earned numerous awards for Personal Sales, #1 recruiter and the #1 Leadership Group Sales in her division for 16 years. She has won trips all across the country and has spoken at many national conventions.

Karen is a Certified Dream Coach® and loves helping others achieve their dreams through coaching. She is also an inspiring speaker and workshop presenter. Her passion is giving hope to others so they can dream again and make their dreams come true, earning the money their families need.

167

Baby or Business

Making Time for You Helps Everyone and Everything Thrive
By Leslie Irish Evans, LMP, NBCR, CA

*C*ongratulations! It's a girl! It's a boy! It's a…limited liability corporation! You're caring for another human being, and you are caring for a business all your own. Stress is something with which you are all too familiar. As a mom entrepreneur, you're working at least two full-time jobs. No wonder you're stressed! Have you ever noticed how much they overlap?

- **Motherhood.** On call around the clock. No breaks. Kids demand constant attention. Thinking of your kids, even when you're away from them. Wondering where all your money went. Nagging fear that you are not doing enough to help your kids reach their highest potential. Envy for other mothers who make it look easy and seem to be having more fun than you. Feeling guilty when you choose to put your needs first.

- **Entrepreneurship.** Always the boss. Business demands your full attention. Thinking about it, even when you're away from it. Any money you make gets poured back into your business. Continuous worry that you're not doing enough to help your business grow. Envy when other businesses thrive and yours does not. Feeling guilty when you take time away from your business.

Either one of these is a demanding and exhausting job. Trying to do both at once can quickly lead to overwhelm, burnout and frustration. What's a mom entrepreneur to do? The answer lies in the graceful art of self-care.

Self-Care

Caring for yourself is a muscle that you might not be accustomed to using. With babies, business, home and spouse, you're probably used to skillfully managing the needs and requirements of everyone except yourself. Yes, yes, you know that you *should* exercise. You know you *should* probably get more sleep. You know that a consistent diet of junk food isn't good for you. "But," you say, "I'm an extremely busy woman! I don't have time for such things!" The truth is that you ignore such things to your own detriment. Self-care is a fundamental necessity for health, happiness and prosperity in both your personal and professional life.

Five Bite-Sized Benefits for Your Bottom Line

Bearing in mind that mom entrepreneurs are extremely busy, I've created a list of five bite-sized self-care tips. The list could easily be longer, and it has been my experience that these five provide the most bang for your buck.

> *"Sleep is the best meditation."*
> —Tenzin Gyatso, the 14th Dalai Lama

Tip #1: Get sufficient sleep. The benefit of getting sufficient sleep is increased energy, reduced anxiety and clearer thinking. As a massage therapist, plenty of stressed-out clients come walking through my door. One of the first things health professionals will look at when assessing a client's lifestyle is sleep. With its hugely restorative ability, it's one of the core factors in taking good care of oneself. Yet, in our go-go society, it's also one of the first things people let go of when they have what seems like too much on their plates.

In the case of new moms, sleep can be hard to come by. Even after the kids are old enough to sleep through the night, many of us still find our sleep disrupted, often due to bad habits we've acquired along the way. Take a look at some of these scenarios and see if any apply to you:

• **Too much caffeine and/or alcohol.** I had a client in my office who was extremely stressed. She had a great deal of personal drama going on in her life and was also working a very challenging job at a large corporation. She said she wasn't sleeping well. Understandable, given the way her life was going at the time. However, when I asked her about her caffeine intake, her answer shocked me. She was having at least six cups of coffee a day! Another client visited me with sleep complaints and told of having three to four glasses of wine every night just before bed.

Caffeine, as we know, is a stimulant. It can also increase anxiety. Alcohol, though often seen as helpful in falling asleep—nightcap anyone?—can actually disrupt sleep patterns and make it difficult to *stay* asleep. Both caffeine and alcohol can wreak havoc on your sleep. Take a look at your consumption of these items and determine whether or not you need to reduce or even eliminate their use.

• **Build transition time into your evening routine.** Would you take your kids out for a run and then immediately toss them in their beds and expect them to fall asleep? Of course not. You know they need time to wind down. You may even have a bedtime routine you do with them such as having a bath, reading a book or taking some quiet time to chat about their day. Yet, do you do the same for yourself, or do you try to cram in as much work as you can before bedtime? Perhaps you watch the evening news—violent and scary—and then shut out the lights. Both of these can keep your mind racing as you lie in bed. Better to shut off all media and engage in some quiet, easy activity before bedtime. Allow your mind to transition from busy to resting and you'll have an easier time falling asleep.

- **Set an alarm for your bedtime.** Picture this: mom entrepreneur extraordinaire Susan Jones gets her kids off to bed, gets the dishes done and sits down at her laptop to do a little online socializing. Knowing she does better with a good night's sleep, she sets an intention of going to bed at 10 p.m. When she looks up from her laptop, it's midnight. "Aaugh!" she cries. "I meant to go to bed two hours ago!" Sound familiar? It can happen to the best of us. As one of my clients told me: "I'm an expert at putting my kids to bed, and not good at all about putting myself to bed."

If you're not very good about putting yourself to bed, try setting an alarm for your bedtime. That's right, not one for waking up, though you may well need that too, but one for going to bed. Use your phone or your computer or a genuine alarm clock to remind yourself that it's time to power down and get some shut-eye.

> *"Please secure your own oxygen mask before assisting others."*
> —Standard safety announcement on commercial air flights

Tip #2: Pay yourself first. The benefit of paying yourself first is peace of mind and decreased resentment. You've heard the above quote on every commercial flight, and it's a sensible guideline. However, have you ever thought about the reasons for it? The literal scenario is this: air cabin loses pressure, oxygen masks drop, panicked mom tries to secure mask on wriggling child and passes out before she is successful. Now we have two people with no oxygen. This is, of course, less than ideal. I was in a group of mothers when this very topic came up and was stunned to hear nearly every mother say they would attempt to secure their child's mask first. "But you'll both die!" I cried. They remained unmoved and said they wouldn't be able to help themselves first.

Thankfully, I have never seen this scenario play out in real life. However, I have seen it played out metaphorically in myriad ways. Stressed-out moms tend to take care of everyone else first, and if you're running your business the same way, you're piling on more stress. Whether we're talking about oxygen, food, rest or money, the best practice is to pay yourself first. Why? Pretty simple, really: the odds of everyone in the group being taken care of increase tremendously when the leader is fit to perform. Try these suggestions on for size and see what works for you:

- Pay yourself money first. "I can't afford to!"—I hear you crying. Hear me out. I'm not advocating you get a full salary while the rent goes unpaid. In the case of your business, I'm talking about putting away something, even just five dollars if that's all you can truly spare, to give yourself something you can watch grow—a measure of your hard work. In the case of your home life, if the kids get an allowance, make sure you get something too. Otherwise you're designating yourself as a second-class citizen in your own family.

- Pay yourself time first. This can be time for rest, time for recreation, time to take care of yourself before you serve others. See Tip #4.

- Pay yourself love first. This may be the most difficult suggestion of all, yet it's the one with the biggest payoff. We're all familiar with The Golden Rule: "Do unto others as you would have them do unto you." I call the following "The Diamond Rule" (because I think it's even more valuable): "Do unto yourself as you would do unto others." How many of us save our kindest behavior for others while brutally criticizing ourselves? Practice holding yourself to the most loving, generous standard of all.

"Refusing to ask for help when you need it is refusing someone the chance to be helpful."
—Ric Ocasek, American musician

Tip #3: Ask for help. The benefit of asking for help is the completion of long-standing "to do" lists, freedom from having to do it all, and mental breathing room. "I'm tired of having to do everything myself!" Sound familiar? True, as a mom entrepreneur you've got a lot of responsibilities. Where is it written that you have to do it all yourself? Is it possible you've fallen into a rut of *choosing* to do everything yourself because you think: a) it's easier, b) it's faster or c) you can't afford not to? Perhaps you're worried about being a burden to others. It's time to reframe this thinking and ask for help.

- **Figure out what you need help with.** You know you're overwhelmed. Yet the question "Anything I can do to help?" often leaves you stymied. What do you need help with? Is it the bookkeeping? The laundry? Grocery shopping? Take a look at your day and figure out which tasks could be farmed out. Remember, a good boss knows how to delegate.

- **Cede control.** "If you want something done right, do it yourself." Have you heard yourself say or think this? However, one person can only do so much. Are you a perfectionist? Does your partner offer to help with the kids or the business, only to have you snatch the job back from him because he's not doing it "right"? Remember this phrase from the French philosopher Voltaire: "Le mieux est l'ennemi du bien," which translates as "The perfect is the enemy of the good." Do you want it perfect or do you want it good and complete? The choice is yours.

- **Consider hiring a professional.** Face it, there are some things you're good at and some things you are not good at. When you are ready to accept that humble reality, consider asking for help from someone who is really good at doing what you need. Home organization? Mental health counseling? Accounting? There are other entrepreneurs out there who are skilled at filling these needs. Afraid you can't afford them? Shop around for prices, consider bartering and take a good hard look at what your health and mental sanity are worth to you. My mother got such mental relief from hiring a cleaning service to come to our house that she would say, "I can pay it to a shrink, or I can pay it to a cleaning service. The results are the same."

"We need quiet time to examine our lives openly and honestly. Spending quiet time alone gives your mind an opportunity to renew itself and create order."
—Susan Taylor, American journalist

Tip #4: Insert white space into your day. The benefit of inserting white spaces into your day is improved focus and reduced burnout. Do you keep a schedule book or use a day planner? Many mom entrepreneurs do. With our various roles of mom, boss, cook, chauffeur and so on, it's important to be able to keep track of "where" and "when." Perhaps you even have it organized into different categories: Home – Kids – Work. However, do you have a "Me" category? Adding white space time to your calendar will assure that you do.

White space is a concept in visual and graphic arts which describes the area not covered with ink or paint. Imagine how crowded this page you're reading right now would look if it were completely covered with letters. The more white space one sees on a page, the more one is able to rest one's eyes and brain and appreciate the areas that are occupied.

Do you see the analogy here? Filling your calendar to the absolute brim is a direct path to diminishing returns. Counterintuitive as it may seem, putting *fewer* things on your schedule increases your efficiency and your productivity. Try the following tips to create more breathing room in your schedule and your life:

- **Block out a chunk of time for yourself on your schedule.** Choose a day, preferably one where your schedule isn't too busy, and block out your time. Try three hours if you can manage it, or only one if that's too difficult. The point is to have a piece of time that is dedicated entirely to nurturing yourself. You must begin this appointment with no predetermined agenda. When it begins, ask yourself, "What do I really need right now?"

- **Honor that time as sacred.** Keeping this commitment to yourself is the hardest part. It will be very tempting to see that empty block on your calendar as a chance to catch up on laundry, sales calls or grocery shopping. Don't do it! This time is for you and your own well-being. Don't send yourself the message that you are disposable.

- **Lather, rinse and repeat.** Once you've done it, do it again. Do it daily, do it weekly, do it whenever you are able. Like self-care, white space time is a muscle that needs regular exercise. For more information on this topic, visit www.whitespacetime.com.

> *"Fall down seven times, get up eight."*
> —Japanese proverb

Tip #5: Seek flexibility and resilience before balance. The benefit of flexibility and resilience is reduced stress, improved adaptability and enhanced serenity. Many of us strive to find the proper work-life balance. What exactly do we mean by that? Is it 50 percent of our time at work and 50 percent at home? Real life simply doesn't work that way. The normal fluctuations of life demand that sometimes work calls us to give more than 50 percent of our time, and sometimes home does the same thing. Keep the following tips in mind when thinking about leading a "balanced" life:

- **Accept the fact that life ebbs and flows.** Most of us realize that life has its ups and downs. Good days and bad days are part of the natural cycle of things. Disruptions and stressors will always be there. It's how we choose to react to them that determines our happiness. Consider the metaphor of a tree in a storm: a perfectly balanced, yet brittle, tree will snap in a hurricane; a flexible tree will bend with the heavy winds and a resilient tree will bounce back up.

- **Consider yoga.** I regularly suggest yoga to my clients to help them become more flexible and resilient. Those of you who practice yoga know that the physical benefits are great, and the mental benefits of practicing calmness and relaxation in the midst of the challenging poses are even greater. Yoga is a metaphor for life.

- **Laugh and move on when things go awry.** Question: How do you make God laugh? Answer: Tell Him your plans. A somewhat cynical joke, perhaps, and a great way to acknowledge that life is bound to take twists and turns that we didn't see coming. "Do what you can and can what you can't" is a useful expression to remember when things don't work out as expected.

Congratulations on being a mom entrepreneur extraordinaire. Despite the challenges listed in this chapter, and the many others you've doubtless experienced first-hand, you know of the rich rewards that both motherhood and being your own boss offer. Your smarts, tenacity, and rich creativity have gotten you this far and will serve you well as you continue on this amazing journey. I applaud your beautiful spirit, and warmly encourage you to regularly nurture yourself with the same loving care you've shown your families and your business. Remember, you are the boss!

Leslie Irish Evans,
LMP, NBCR, CA

(425) 445-3759
leslie@leslieirishevans.com
www.leslieirishevans.com
www.peelingmomofftheceiling.com

"Mommy Martyrs No More!" is the rallying cry Leslie Irish Evans shares to empower moms in the midst of the madness of modern motherhood to find peace, calm and purpose—no matter what. A modern-day Erma Bombeck who offers quick wit and powerful truth, Leslie's popular radio program, workshops, keynote presentations, blog posts and articles touch hearts and shape formerly crazy lives for the better. Invite Leslie to contribute to your upcoming conference, workshop, or radio program. Touching lives in one profound way or another has been Leslie's passion for years.

Leslie's show, *Peeling Mom Off the Ceiling*, can be heard on radio stations around the country every Monday via the I'm Thankful Network. In addition, she is a licensed massage therapist, a nationally board-certified reflexologist and a former harried mom who has embraced her own advice to successfully guide hundreds of others to do the same. She quips that she's been "peeling moms off the ceiling since 2006, one mommy martyr at a time." There is plenty more good work to do before her mission is complete.

Look Like a Rock Star as You Blog Your Way to Success

By Holly Chantal, M.Ed.

*O*ne of my favorite things about using a website for marketing is that whether you are new or established in your business, you can make yourself look like an expert. The best way to do this is through a blog. Many people cringe when they hear the "B" word because they think it's too much work, there's too much hype about it, or they don't know what to write about. I can assure you that starting a blog will be the best thing you can do to market your business on the Internet. In this chapter you will not only learn how to blog, you will also learn how to position yourself through your website and blog so that you look like a rock star.

Why Your Website Needs a Blog

• Your blog establishes you as an expert in your field because you will provide content to your target audience that speaks directly to their needs and desires.

• A professional-looking blog can make you look like a celebrity, even if you've only been in business for a short time.

• You can build a relationship with visitors through their comments, and by writing posts that directly relate to their needs and desires.

- You can use your blog to promote special events, teleseminars or product launches.

- Blogs are rich in keywords, making your website rank higher in search engines and driving targeted traffic to your website.

- Blogs are dynamic! You can include articles, podcasts and videos, so that no matter what medium your audience prefers, they will find it in your blog.

- Articles written for your blog can be distributed to article banks as well as other blogs and websites, which will increase your visibility and reach.

- Your articles can be repurposed later if you decide to write a book. You can also use them to write courses, record them into podcasts or turn them into teleclasses and videos.

- Blogs are free!

A blog is very easy to add to your website. I recommend Wordpress®, which is already integrated with most hosting services. Wordpress is amazing because it's set up perfectly for search engine optimization (SEO). Its design flexibility is incredible, it's free, and you can install plug-ins and widgets that give you control over every aspect of your website without having to hire someone. If you prefer, you can hire someone to help you set up your blog and give you advice on template formats and widgets. After that, it is easy for you to post new entries. Wordpress makes it all very simple.

Setting Up a Schedule

One of the hardest things about maintaining a blog is being consistent. However, as with anything in your business, consistency is the key to getting results. The first thing you need to decide is how often you are going to post. Three times a week is ideal, and that can be quite a daunting prospect for someone starting out. You can start out posting once or twice a week and then, once you have the hang of it and are consistent, simply add more posts each week. Just make sure that once you commit to a number, you stick to it! If your audience doesn't think you are taking your blog seriously, then they are going to stop paying attention.

The other step you will want to take is to set up a writing schedule for yourself. Set aside time during your week to write your posts and then schedule them to be published at future dates. You can even schedule posts to keep rolling out while you and the kids are vacationing.

It is also a good idea to set up an editorial calendar. Basically, this is a breakdown of what you will write about week to week or month to month. It will ensure that you always have something to write. If you set it all up in advance, you will have a much easier time in the long run. For example, if you're an accountant, here's a possible editorial calendar schedule:

- In January you'll want to write about getting your tax return in early.

- In February and March, maybe you'll write more about tax preparation.

- After tax season, you could write about optimizing your finances so you can save up for a summer vacation.

- Near school season, you could write about investment accounts to save for future college tuition.

- In the fall, you can write about the holidays.

Beyond making an editorial calendar, you can break down your schedule to make it even easier to come up with topics. For instance, if you want to post three times a week, you could break it up:

- On Mondays, write about whatever topic is hot at the time or corresponds to your editorial calendar.

- On Wednesdays, spotlight a product or service that is your own or that of a referral partner.

- On Fridays, you can read a past article into your audio recorder and post it as a podcast.

In this scenario, you're really only creating new content once a week, yet you're posting three times a week. It doesn't seem so hard anymore, does it?

What to Write About

Writer's block is a scary thing and it stops a lot of successful entrepreneurs in their tracks when it comes to starting a blog or newsletter. You will start noticing that you run across topics every day, and once you start writing, you'll find that topics will just pop into your head consistently throughout the day. Keep a notebook or even a 3x5 card handy to capture these spur-of-the-moment ideas.

To get you started, here is a great way to figure out what you can write about that will establish you as an expert right off the bat and serve your target audience. The trick is to determine these two things:

- What are the urgent needs of your target market? Urgent needs are anything that your customers are trying to move away from. They're the things they complain about, search for solutions for and in general, just do not like or want to deal with anymore.

- What are the compelling desires of your target market? Compelling desires are the results that your customer is moving toward, hopefully as a result of using your product or service.

You can find great examples of both of these principles everywhere. If you really want to take a crash course in urgent needs and compelling desires, watch an infomercial. I actually recommend to my clients that they record infomercials in the early hours of the morning so that they can watch them later and take notes.

Here is an example from an advertisement for Liquid Leather™ on www.asseenontv.com.

- Urgent need: You have an unsightly hole in your car seat or jacket, or something of similar material. You can't afford to have someone fix it. You are worried that the patch will be visible if you fix it yourself. You don't have the tools to fix it yourself.

- Compelling desire: You want something that repairs leather, vinyl and a variety of other materials. It works on mixed colors so that you get a seamless finish. The texture boards are reusable and the package is inexpensive. It includes everything you need to fix the tear with professional results. Plus, you get a bonus fabric repair kit!

Now, if you have a hole in your leather car seat, I bet this sounds pretty tempting. The next time you see a commercial or ad and you think to yourself that you'd like to buy whatever they're selling, see if you can identify the urgent needs and compelling desires that they are playing on.

Once you get the hang of it, you will begin to see urgent needs and compelling desires everywhere on websites and in promotional emails. Try to identify where the writer is playing on an urgent need or a compelling desire and you will start to see how you can do the same thing with your marketing.

Now take a moment to identify your target market's urgent needs and compelling desires. Each urgent need and compelling desire can easily be turned into a title for a blog post, an article or a category for your posts. Now all you need to do is write the blog or article, focusing on the problem or outlining the desired results your target audience seeks.

Writing articles and blogs that speak to these topics will drive targeted traffic to your website because, when people are searching online for solutions, they will be pointed to your blog.

A helpful resource that is great for creating attention-grabbing titles is www.rackandwrite.com. All you do is fill in the blanks with your keywords, your target audience and other relevant information. Then the title engine will list over a hundred titles using those words. This is also a great tool to help you decide what to write about based on the titles that come up when you enter your keywords.

Also, be sure to use this information in all of your marketing materials, such as print ads, brochures, business cards and even the tagline or title of your website. This information is not only great for helping you build your website and book more clients. It can also be used for increasing your sales. Incorporating urgent needs and compelling desires into your sales conversations will help your products or services sell themselves. Chances are, you already talk a lot about the benefits of using your product or service, and these principles give you a clearer picture of just how important they are to your target audience.

Get to the Top of Search Engines for Visibility

Your ability to be found by your target audience is just as important as knowing where to find them, if not more so. Search engine optimization can be a totally complicated science that people pay a lot of money to have done to their website—and it doesn't have to be like that. With just a few simple strategies you can organically drive traffic to your website and increase your website ranking. It may take some patience, yet with consistency you will see yourself at the top of Google®—and not because you paid someone to trick the hamster that powers Google rankings. Your website will not just show up for your target audience. Every piece of your website will compellingly whisper to them.

The first thing you need to do is choose the keywords that will guide your target audience to your web presence. Be sure that the words you choose speak to their urgent needs and compelling desires. For example, if we go back to the leather repair kit above, keywords or phrases you might research would be: how to fix hole in car seat, inexpensive leather repair, matching car seat color. You can do this easily by going to: www.adwords.google.com/select/KeywordToolExternal.

When trying to find your keywords, try entering the name of your target audience, their urgent needs, compelling desires, groups to which they belong, and so on. You can even look up the keywords that your competitors use.

This tool is going to give you a list of relevant keywords, how often they are searched for in a month and how much competition is vying for attention on that keyword. A good rule of thumb is to look for keywords that are searched for around 10,000 times a month and don't have a ridiculous amount of competition. When you are searching for keywords using all of this material, try to find the ones that overlap and choose no more than five to focus on in your website content.

You are going to use these keywords in everything you write for your website. When a search engine crawls your website, it is indexing every piece of text—everything from your domain name and the title of your page, down to your footer at the bottom. It's important that your keywords are in the title of your website and your subtitle. You will use keywords in titles of posts, subtext of photos, as tags and categories in your blog. Basically, anywhere you can type something, you are going to use your keywords. By doing this you are telling the search engines that your website is relevant to those people searching for these words.

You will find that this will come naturally since you will be using the keywords in your posts and pages anyway, and they are relevant to your topics. Try not to worry about it too much. Do keep this list on your desk though, so that when you are writing you can be sure you are using them.

How to Take the Internet by Storm and Show Up Everywhere

Something else that search engines look for when ranking your website is where else your content and web address is mentioned, whether the place that your website is mentioned is relevant to your target audience and whether it is ranked high as well. This all sounds very complicated and it just means that if your friend, who also serves your target audience, refers to your website, the search engine notices and says, "Hey! This woman must know what she's talking about!"

Here are a few ways to get your website and content listed in multiple places so that you start to saturate the Internet with your presence:

- **Post to ezine article directories.** One of the most popular of these is www.ezinearticles.com. You'll find that when you Google just about anything, an ezine article will come up. By posting to these directories, your content is now going to show up in multiple places. Plus, they allow you to add a resource box that has your compelling offer and a link to your website. Other bloggers and ezine writers use these banks for material. Therefore, if you have a good article, it may be frequently picked up and posted elsewhere, along with your resource box. This will add to your website ranking, and also add to your credibility as someone who knows what she's talking about.

- **Find other blogs and forums** that serve your target audience where you can make thoughtful comments and include your link.

- **Record your articles into podcasts** and post them onto podcast directories.

- **Register your blog in blog directories.**

- **List your newsletter** at www.bestezines.com, which is run by the same company as www.ezinearticles.com.

- **Integrate your blog** with your social media networks.

- **Ask friends or colleagues** who serve your target audience if you can exchange blog posts and include a resource box which will help you build links back to your website.

If you do all of these things, you are going to start to build a lot of traffic very quickly, and it's all going to be targeted to your keywords.

Once it's all set up, almost everything is automatic, taking no extra time on your part.

As you can see, having a rock star website isn't as difficult as it seems, and having a blog makes it even easier! Start taking action now, work through these steps, and you can establish a solid web presence and make yourself looks like the go-to expert in your industry, no matter how long you've been in business. In fact, the earlier you start with these strategies the better, because your credibility and web presence will only build over time. Enjoy, and I wish you the best of luck!

Holly Chantal, M.Ed.

**Book Yourself Solid Coach® and
Internet marketing expert**

(207) 380-5691
holly@hollychantal.com
www.hollychantal.com

Holly is a Book Yourself Solid Coach who enjoys helping mom entrepreneurs and coaches use their business as a vehicle for achieving their dreams.

Holly does this through her unique website design and Internet marketing program that helps her clients craft their online brand identity, establish their web presence, and ultimately book more clients. When clients finish working with her, they not only have a dynamic website, they also have success plans to keep them moving forward toward booked-solid bliss.

Holly understands how to balance a business and the responsibilities of being a mother, even if she isn't yet one herself. When Holly isn't teaching others how to market like superstars, she is a "mom" to 30 teenage ballet dancers with whom she resides and who she keeps on track to achieve their own dreams of professional dancing.

If you are looking for a way to bring in more clients using resources you already have and leaving you more time to spend with your family, Holly encourages you to consider using a blog as mentioned in her chapter, or checking out her website for more marketing tips.

The Magic of Event Marketing

Skyrocket Your Business with Successful Events

By Hope Desroches

A hard-working mom deserves to have her business in the spotlight, and a great way to do that is through event marketing. These days, business is about more than having a great product or service. Mom entrepreneurs need to be involved in the community and build real-life connections. Event marketing helps you do this. It is focused on face-to-face interactions through live events and is one of the fastest ways to reach out to the community because it provides the opportunity to get people excited and involved in your business. This chapter will show you how hosting an event or participating in a community festival can build customer loyalty, increase brand awareness and generate excitement about your business.

Event marketing is more effective than traditional advertising because it is non-intrusive and allows you to speak directly to prospective customers. Guests at the event will be open to learning about the event's hosts and sponsors; this makes them easily approachable. Those with whom you speak will remember you in the future because they have met you and learned a little about your business.

I will cover two types of event marketing for small business owners in this chapter: hosting an event and sponsoring one. The advantage of sponsoring is the ability to fully participate and grow your brand without the work required for coordinating and hosting a full event. The advantage of hosting is the opportunity to plan a festival, trade show or meeting exclusively for your preferred audience, plus the option of generating income.

Event planning requires you to take an idea and turn it into something tangible. The information in this chapter should help you in creating your ideal event. If the commitment seems overwhelming, consider hiring a professional planner to help with as much—or as little—as you need.

> *"If you don't have a plan for yourself,*
> *you'll be a part of someone else's."*
> —American proverb

Hosting an Event

The ideal event to host is a "recipe" with five basic, equally important steps. Using each step will make the planning easy and exciting. Ignoring any of these steps could result in an unsuccessful event.

The ingredients of a successful event recipe are:

Step One: Determine the event concept, structure and budget. In this first step, you lay out the blueprint for your event. You have many decisions to make, and putting together a detailed plan will make the planning go smoothly. What are your main objectives? What is the purpose? Do you want to solidify relationships with existing customers or bring in new customers? Will you invite sponsors? What is the best location? How many people will attend? Will there be food or refreshments? Write out all your ideas, then you can choose the best ones for your plan.

Create a solid budget and include all the expenses you will incur for your event. This should include, among other things, items such as marketing, facility, food, security, decorations, refreshments and travel expenses. Developing a budget and sticking to it will save you money because expenses can quickly become overwhelming if you are not prepared.

If one of your objectives is to profit from the event, compare projected expenses to potential profit and, if needed, make adjustments. For example, if you need to sell 200 tickets to make a profit, make sure you have secured a venue that will comfortably fit 200 people.

Be creative while planning and choose a title that draws people into the event. Develop a theme related to your business that will appeal to your audience. For example, a bookstore could host story time, a health professional could organize a wellness exposition, a clothing designer could host a fall fashion fling or a dog groomer could host a pet parade.

Include a fun incentive to entice people to attend. Consider giving back to your local community by hosting a raffle and donating the proceeds to your favorite charity. That charity may also be willing to provide volunteers to help with the event in exchange for your donation. Other ideas you could use to draw a crowd to your event would be free promotional gifts, low-cost activities, performances and live music. If you can offer something to the community that directly relates to your business, such as free samples of your product or service, do so.

Step Two: Establish event programming and scheduling. People come to your event for a purpose, mostly to have a good time. Offer a seamless flow of activities and presenters and provide opportunities to socialize and have fun. Most events do not require too many activities. Provide a schedule for participants to look at and see what is fun and exciting.

If you are hiring speakers or performers, make sure to check their references and, if possible, hear them speak before your event. A poor speaker or performer can negatively affect the entire event and reflect poorly on your business. Discuss timing with performers, and let them know they need to stay on schedule. Activities you have promoted for a certain time should take place on time. This will allow attendees to enjoy everything you have planned for them.

Distribute a program to each attendee to eliminate the need for extra banners or scheduling notices. This is also another opportunity to promote your business. Make sure you include a brief description of your product or service and offer an "event special." This will encourage attendees to keep the program and take advantage of your special.

Step Three: Include vendor and exhibit sales. Sponsors and vendors add value to all types of events. Not including them is leaving money on the table. It can be easy to find sponsors and vendors if you start early. Assemble an appealing sponsor and vendor packet to entice prospective business owners to participate. It should include a unique, valuable sponsorship opportunity. You may want to offer them an area to promote their business on-site, a banner in a high traffic area, their logo and web link on your website or the opportunity to provide promotional items for door prizes.

Begin contacting your prospective sponsors and vendors early and give them the opportunity to plan for themselves. The best vendors have a non-competing business with a target market similar to yours. Keep in mind, most businesses are contacted several times a week about sponsorship opportunities. Set your event apart from the rest by clearly explaining the advantages of participating in *your* event. Be specific and include the number of people you expect to attend, the other vendors invited to participate, what activities will take place and the expected audience. Limit the number of vendors from the same industry in order to ensure everyone's success.

Step Four: Market the event. The key to event marketing is building buzz around it. How can you get people excited about attending your event? Ideally, your marketing will be compelling and cost-effective.

Each event you host should have its own logo and web page. These two things comprise the center of your marketing. The logo should grab the attention of your target market and be consistent on all your marketing materials. It is fine to give your event a page on your business's website as long as potential attendees have a place where they can find all the details and can register, if necessary.

Distribute posters and fliers around the community and let people know about the event. Include an attention grabber and target your audiences with an enticing phrase like, "An Event Just for Women" or "Fun for the Whole Family." Make sure you include the following information: your business name and contact phone number, website address, the event logo and logistics, such as the address of the venue, the start and end times of the event, a full list of activities, and so on.

Working with media sponsors is much more effective than traditional advertising, and it allows you to get exposure from the same media outlets from which you might otherwise have to buy ads. Consumers are intrigued by an article in the newspaper or an on-air radio interview about an exciting, upcoming event. This can also benefit media sponsors if you offer them the opportunity to promote themselves at your event.

Start looking for media sponsors by writing a press release that grabs their attention. When writing this press release, think of yourself as a news reporter. What information would you be interested in publicizing? Answer the who, what, where, when, why and how of your event.

After you write the press release, call local newspapers, radio stations and television stations to tell them about the event. Communicate with passion and excitement before asking if you may send a press release.

Lastly, an important step in event marketing is creating online buzz. Post frequent updates on all your social media sites. Ask your contacts to share your event page with their online following. Sharing the event and asking others to do so is vital. Be sure vendors and sponsors also promote the event to their clients. Prepare an email they can easily forward to their contacts.

Step Five: Manage logistics and staffing. This step requires attention to detail. Event logistics covers everything from making sure the napkins are nicely arranged on the food table to ordering enough water glasses to mopping up spills. This is where an event host or organizer needs to delegate and become an event manager.

Depending on the size of the event, hire staff or recruit friends to help with logistics. Forgetting or ignoring seemingly meaningless tasks can result in an event that is considered less than impressive.

As an event manager, your first duty is to create a detailed checklist of everything that needs to be done for the event and make sure each person on your team has a few responsibilities from this list. Do not miss anything, especially little things like decorations, beverages and toiletries.

Extra Bonus Step: Serve and enjoy. You did it! If you follow this recipe, you should create a perfect event for your business.

The day of the event may feel stressful, and you have done the best you can. At this point, smile, have fun and use these tips to build relationships with attendees.

After the event, ask how you can use these steps to be even more successful next time. Review revenues and costs against your budget, and accomplishments against goals.

> *"What is there more kindly than*
> *the feeling between host and guest?"*
> —Aeschylus, Greek poet

Sponsoring an Event

When you sponsor an event, you assist in financing it in exchange for a vendor booth or other publicity. It eliminates the pressure of planning and hosting the entire thing. Vendor fairs, festivals and trade shows are excellent opportunities to network with other businesses and expand your customer base. No matter how large or small the event, you can use the following information to be a successful sponsor.

Your primary goal is to make lasting relationships. You need a way of following up with the people you meet at the event. Busy attendees may not buy your product and may not make any kind of commitment to follow up with you. It is your job to follow up with them. Building a business relationship with the people you meet means being there when they are ready to say yes to your offer.

Your space at a festival or trade show is your storefront for the day. Use that space to get people excited about your business. Make it look as exciting and inviting as possible. A raffle or giveaway is always a big hit. This will draw people in and give you the opportunity to have them complete a registration form. Tell visitors they need to fill out the entire form to be entered into the drawing. Include a box they can check to be added to your mailing list. Once you have captured their information, you can build relationships and market to them for years to come.

Ideally, you can do business on the spot and build relationships at the same time. To increase sales, prepare a special offer for the event, giving attendees an incentive to buy or to commit to buy at the event. Offer a discount on your service for that day only or give them a free product with a purchase. You may want to get a deposit for future services.

Smile and greet everyone. Treat everyone with good manners and excitement. The people you meet came to have fun, so be the life of the party. Offer genuine compliments and be open to brief conversations. Simply being nice and having a positive attitude is your most important asset.

The Profit Is in the Follow-Up

"Regardless of how you feel inside, always try to look like a winner. Even if you are behind, a sustained look of control and confidence can give you a mental edge that results in victory."
—Diane Arbus, American photographer

Whether you are sponsoring or hosting your own event, the key to success is follow-up. In the week after the event, call everyone you met and invite them to do business with you.

Make notes about each person you call. Call them back if they are not home or are unable to speak with you.

Add everyone to your mailing list—get permission when they sign up for the event—in order to keep them current on new services and specials. If someone does not show interest in your business at that time, continue developing your relationship with him or her in a respectful way. You never know when someone will refer your next best customer to you or become that customer.

Event marketing can skyrocket your business because of the strong connections you will develop in the community. Strong connections will increase your contacts and revenues. It is a form of marketing that allows you to build trust in a personal, intimate way, and gives you the opportunity to develop life-long customers. If you are ready to become a celebrity in your field and be recognized and respected for your hard work, plan an event and start using this recipe for success today!

Hope Desroches

Sell it Events

Events and occasions just right for your business

(925) 848-5966

hope@sellitevents.com

www.sellitevents.com

Hope is, above all, a mother of two. She started her business, Sell it Events, with the goal of fulfilling her professional passion and staying home with her children. Hope is an expert in event marketing. She has organized many successful trade shows and festivals, managing every detail from start to finish. She sets her events above the standard by offering exciting event elements that are attractive to the target market. These include partnerships with nonprofit organizations, planned activities and live performances at most events.

As an event marketer, Hope Desroches has helped many business owners get onto the center stage. She can create an event and help companies of any size reach their target market, or activate current sponsorships. She takes care of all the logistics, from negotiation, marketing and vendors, all the way through to follow-up. Her dedication to each event and every client she works with makes her a pleasure to work with.

Use Networking to Build Your Business through Relationships

By Patti Snyders-Blok

"It's not what you know but
who you know that makes the difference."
—Author Unknown

$\mathcal{M}$any mom entrepreneurs think networking means talking to strangers about your business, which for some is a scary thought. Networking is more about building relationships than building business—and building relationships is something most mom entrepreneurs know how to do!

The suggestions I offer in this chapter are mostly from my personal success in multilevel marketing. Regardless of your business, you will discover many ways you can use networking to build relationships that enhance both your business and your life.

What Is Networking?

When mothers open a business, they often do not open a storefront business, rent space or buy advertising. Most mothers work out of their homes and need word-of-mouth advertising and referrals to promote their work. Networking in the right circles is both a free and a professional way of advertising your business. When you network, you let others know what you do, and how your business can help them.

Networking is the exchange of information or services. Start by asking other business owners about their businesses. Learning how you can help them succeed helps your relationship with them grow. Once you have learned how you can help them, they will want to know how they can help you. By working together, you help both businesses.

Networking also creates excitement around your business. This excitement will create "buzz." People will start talking about your business, which can lead to a wider circle of influence.

Imagine your business name going out to every customer of a local hair salon. Networking with the owner of the hair salon to get his name out to your customers in other neighborhoods may be just what he needs. Offering coupons to each of his customers may start conversations with your business in mind.

Where Can a Mom Entrepreneur Network?

Networking within the relationships you have already built is the easiest type of networking. A good place to start is with your own circle of influence—your family, your friends, your family's friends or extended family, your children's school or daycare, your social clubs, and so on. Make a list of everyone you know who might be interested in your business. Now, expand your list to include people you don't yet know, and who might be interested in your business. Don't forget about social networking sites such as moms' groups on Facebook® or Yahoo®. All of these are good ways to get your business known.

Remember, networking is not just about you. Look at what you can offer and how you can get involved in a meaningful way:

- Offer some items from your business as door prizes for group meetings or as small gifts to the moms in the soccer club.

- Speak at local meetings. Give people information they can use while showing them how what you do can benefit their lives.

- Get known as the "jewelry lady," the "skin care mom" or the "family life coach."

Build Your Network Circle

I attended a conference in Chicago and learned from Bob Burg that the average network circle is between 200-300 people. These are people who know you and trust you. When you call them, they are happy to hear from you.

Use the FRANK method to jog your memory and identify everyone in your network circle. This acronym stands for:

- Friends

- Relatives

- Associates or acquaintances

- Neighbors

- Kid's contacts

Get out your address book and start making your list.

How Many People Can You Reach?

If your network circle is 200 people, let's assume each of your family members' and friends' networks are around 200 people—with some overlap, of course. Assuming each of your 200 contacts knows 200 other people, your total potential network circle is around 40,000 people!

That's a big number. You may wonder, "Can I really benefit from all of those people?" How many people you can benefit from will depend on your target audience—the people to whom you want to market your business's products and services. Let's assume your target market is women between the ages of 25 and 50. Half of your network circle will probably be female, and maybe one-third of that will be your target audience. This brings the number down to around 7,000. This is an exciting number of people, definitely worth exploring.

Now that you know how many people you can reach through networking in your circle, you need to figure out how to offer your services in other network circles.

How Can You Fit into
Someone Else's Network Circle?

Fitting yourself into another's network circle will depend on what you are offering and how you offer it. Let's say you are doing a client or hostess appreciation event and want to serve cake to over 100 women. However, your budget will not stretch that far. You could invite a local bakery to help you. Let the bakery know you are entertaining 100 women and explain that this would be a good opportunity for them to show off their specialty cakes. They could have a table set up and serve cupcakes as samples. This would help their business by advertising at a local event. In addition, you would thank the bakery in front of your audience and promote their business during the event.

Another way of fitting into others' network circles is to look for businesses that are similar to yours and not direct competitors. For example, if you sell children's books, you and the bakery in the previous example could partner to advertise both of your products to young mothers as a birthday package.

Any business with a regular clientele has its own network circle. Even small, home-based businesses have databases. If you have a party plan business, do you have any friends who also do home parties? Combining parties for a VIP sale would bring both your databases together to benefit each other. You will have new people from which to draw new energy and you also will have someone you trust supporting you.

What is your target audience? How can you reach them within your own network circle and through other network circles?

Do Networking Circles Get Saturated?

Like any part of business, your circle of influence, or a business with which you have aligned yourself, will get saturated. If you were setting up a drawing box in a local gym to collect names for your database, at some point all interested people in the gym would have entered your drawing and have been contacted. You will start seeing the same names entered again. This is a good indication to move on to another business with your drawing box. Your business will benefit more by networking with another company to keep your database full of fresh leads. Your business lives and breathes and needs fresh air from time to time. Even though the air you're breathing is keeping your business alive, you may want some fresh air to revitalize the energy within your business.

Think about your target audience. Always work with businesses or network circles where your business will directly benefit. Your target clientele should always be the deciding factor.

How Can Networking Grow Your Business?

You will find that through networking, your business can grow very fast. If you use your own network circle or your extended network circle, you may be limited in the people you want to reach with your business. I urge you to think about a bigger picture. I was a stay-at-home mom with a strongly religious extended family when I chose Passion Parties® as my business. Passion Parties are home parties with romance enhancement products. Since my network circle was somewhat limited, I needed to take a wider approach. I contacted wedding planners, and given that everyone wanted a fun get-together with their friends before the wedding, bachelorette parties were my first choice. I marketed myself as entertainment. Before long, my Rare Passions business was thriving. What businesses could you consider networking with to build circles of influence that are outside your usual way of thinking?

Once I started my search for other opportunities, I also targeted complementary businesses that served the audience I wanted to attract. The results were huge. I soon had more parties than I could personally attend to, which made it easier to attract new team members. Leading by example, my team members have also grown their businesses through networking with wedding fairs, trade shows and local clubs.

No matter what business you are in, there are many kinds of networking. You can move your business forward if you network both within and outside your industry. I network with other companies, within my company, within my immediate family, and with other leaders and consultants as well.

> *"The best prospect is the client who has already dealt with you. The second best is the one referred to you by a client who has dealt with you previously. The third best is the one referred to you by another trusted professional or friend."*
> —Marilyn Jennings, Canadian author and speaker

Network within your family. Your immediate family is the most important place to start creating a strong network. When your family is involved in your business, you have the full support of your spouse and children and you can work your business guilt-free. Share your goals with your family and explain how they will help the entire family when you attain them. The main reason I started Rare Passions was to spend more time with my family. Therefore, sharing the benefits with my family is my primary goal.

My family is the heart of my business. My husband is the vice president of Rare Passions, and my two children are on the board of directors. We make all business decisions together. When our goals are reached, we share the rewards with family first.

Network within your company or industry. Before I had a team of Rare Passion Divas working with me, I asked other Passion Parties consultants to work with me. These other business owners helped me become the leader I am today. Now that my team is 200 members strong, when a large trade show is secured, we work together and benefit as a team by sharing leads from the show. This demonstrates strength in numbers to your team members and shows new, potential consultants how teamwork can help them with their new businesses.

The Rare Passion Divas have also put together large appreciation events and product launches. You benefit from the guests you invite, as do your team members, and everyone benefits from the energy created. Although the energy from 20 people can be strong, the energy from 200 is much stronger!

Working with other business owners can give you the knowledge and experience you need when you are trying something for the first time. In return, you can help their businesses by offering your success tips to them.

Network with other businesses. This is almost always beneficial to both companies. Here are some possible ways to collaborate:

- Work with other business owners to expose your products to their clientele and vice versa.

- Ask other businesses to bring their products to one of your hostess appreciation events. You advertise for them and gain free products to use as gifts at your presentation. They do the same for you.

- Give numerous door prizes to community events to gain exposure for your business and to help them raise money.

- Help fellow business owners by sharing your expertise and advice.

The network relationships you build are appreciated by other businesses, and the more helpful you are, the more helpful they will be in return.

Network with strangers. Cold calling and attending trade shows are two activities that are considered networking with strangers.

Cold calling is the process of contacting prospective clients who are not expecting your sales call and may not know you. I have found cold calling makes most mom entrepreneurs uncomfortable. Collecting referrals from people in your network circle, on the other hand, is usually more profitable and easier to do. Referrals are an amazing way to build your business fast since you are being recommended by someone whom the prospect trusts.

Trade shows can build your clientele as well, and you must work the leads you get and build relationships in a short amount of time. One way to do this is to offer a door prize. Give door prize slips to each person who visits your table at the trade show. After talking to someone who shows interest in your products or services, add a note to his or her door prize slip to jog your memory. You might write, "Young lady with beautiful baby girl." This will help you when you make follow-up phone calls after the show. Your new clients will be amazed you remembered them.

Use social networking. Social networks are groups that focus on building relationships among people who share the same interests. Most of these are Internet or web-based services. The most popular ones are Facebook, Twitter®, MySpace® and LinkedIn®. It is important to separate your personal information from your business information. In other words, have a specific social network just for business. This will help keep the boundaries clear.

Networking Means More than Business

> *"Eighty percent of life's satisfaction comes from meaningful relationships."*
> —Brian Tracy, American best-selling author
> and professional speaker

I have become very successful at building my Rare Passion business. I have also built many amazing personal relationships through networking. The friends I have met through my business, within my Rare Passion team, within the Passion Party sisterhood and beyond, are the best friends I could have ever asked for. Not only have they helped me through referrals and worked alongside me at huge events, they have helped me to grow into the leader I am today. Gaining mutual respect and admiration through our continuous business ventures has been invaluable for all the businesses involved.

I urge you to go out and network within your circle and find your target audience through other businesses and in your friends' network circles. Build your business by building relationships and helping other business owners build theirs.

Patti Snyders-Blok

Passion Parties® Executive Director

(403) 273-5841
patti@rarepassions.com
www.rarepassions.com

Patti Snyders-Blok is married to John Snyders-Blok and they are the proud parents of two beautiful girls, Kendra and Alyssa. Patti's business keeps her busy on the weekends and allows her to continue being a full-time mom. This also enables her to be an active participant in her daughters' school, as well as to volunteer on a weekly basis at her local zoo.

As an Executive Director of Passion Parties, Patti manages a team of over 200 women. She motivates and coaches them to move their businesses forward toward their own goals.

Patti has been with Passion Parties since 2004, and she loves her business. She is on the Executive Director Council and has achieved her car qualification bonus. She takes incredible business trips and amazing family vacations, and has the financial freedom to enjoy luxuries that seemed unattainable in the past. Her Passion Parties family is the most amazing network of friends, filled with relationships that will last a lifetime.

Patti attributes her success to believing in the words of Jack Canfield, "Act as if…" Her words of advice to other mom entrepreneurs are, "Act as if it were impossible to fail and your dreams can come true."

Finding and Working with Mentors to Create Success

By Schall Adams

If you want anything more out of life, you must first get more out of yourself. A mentor can help you do just that.

How often have you had great dreams and visions for your life, then when you started moving toward them, you hit a roadblock and just gave up? Most of us have been in that place at one point or another. Perhaps you are in that place now. In this chapter, I will share with you how, with the assistance of mentors, you can create anything you desire. All it takes is reaching out and asking for help.

A mentor is an experienced and trusted advisor, someone who can share knowledge with you that you do not currently possess. They can open you up to a world of ideas that you do not even know exists. A mentor has the skills to lead you through the steps you need to take to create unimaginable success in your life with ease, clarity and grace. Your ideas will grow by leaps and bounds with the right mentor and you will be amazed at all of the possibilities. If you are looking to grow or expand in any area of your life, then finding the right mentor can help you reach your goals much sooner.

My Story

I have always had an entrepreneurial spirit. When I became a young, single mother, it became even more important to me to create a business as an asset that would give me the freedom to spend time with my son. I also wanted to create the resources for him to be able to start his adult life on his own terms.

For so many years, I struggled with trying to create my own business, yet I never produced the results I was looking for. I always needed to work a regular job, too. Now I can look back at my efforts and see the biggest mistake I made during that time was trying to do it alone without the help of mentors.

Finally, in 2006, I found the wisdom and the courage to seek the assistance of others. I quit my corporate job and just went for it. At first, I constantly read and listened to informative and motivational books and CDs. This was a good first step and brought me some success. Then I began to search out mentors more aggressively. I hired a personal coach, enrolled in several training programs and joined a very successful group of businesswomen who network together and support each other in a variety of ways. After attending the annual conference for this women's group, I enrolled in several of the women's programs and also began working with a buddy coach from the group.

Working with these mentors catapulted my success in ways that I could never have imagined. It took me from being immersed in the struggle to becoming a great achiever. In less than one year, I became a co-author of a motivational book and signed to co-author a second book. I also signed with a publishing house for my own book and CD series, recorded a music CD with my own blues band, created a program that teaches people to build their own raw food and healthy living business, began speaking professionally around the country, and founded an organization to help women from around the globe mentor each other.

I share my story with you because I want to show you how important mentors are in our lives. Especially as mom entrepreneurs, we have a tendency to think we can do it all. The "supermom" syndrome. We cannot do it all. No one can. We need each other to *really* soar above the ordinary and reach new heights.

The Importance of Working with Mentors

Deciding to grow or to achieve something new in life is a decision that many people make. Perhaps you have made this decision in the past yourself, only to have it end in disappointment. Here are four important reasons why finding a mentor is important in helping you achieve success with any new endeavor:

• **Mentors have skills.** A mentor is someone who has skills that you do not. Like everyone, you have areas where you need to grow and develop. Having the advantage of his or her specialized knowledge, a mentor can guide you in building your skills faster than you could do so alone. They have developed the very skills you need and they often wish to share them to help others grow and expand.

• **Mentors have experience.** A mentor is someone who has experience that you likely do not. They are several steps ahead in the game you want to play. Because they have already been through it, a mentor has knowledge that helps you avoid certain mistakes. They understand the rules of the road and they can draw you a map. Through their experiences they have developed an understanding of what does and does not work. They have been there and know the way. You can learn quite a bit from their experience.

• **Mentors can keep you moving.** A mentor is someone who can help get you going when you stall out. Even very successful people get stuck from time to time. It makes perfect sense that this would happen, because you cannot always be "on." Connecting with your mentor can help you discover why you are stalling out and provide the motivation you need to break through to another level or discover the reason for the block so that you can remove it.

- **Mentors can share resources.** A mentor is someone who can share resources that you do not know about. Remember, this person is several steps ahead and therefore knows the reliable resources you need for the next steps in your life.

Two Main Kinds of Mentors

There are different kinds of mentors. Here are two approaches I use when I want to work one-on-one with a professional or expert in my field.

- **Ask for mentoring.** You can sometimes find people who have expertise in an area you wish to learn about who will share some of their time with you. They may agree to have a couple of conversations with you about their experiences and guide you to a good starting point. Once you have found some experts you think have the experience you want, contact them and ask if you can take them to lunch. Let them know that you would like to ask a few questions about their expertise. There are many people who will do this because it is another way for them to make a difference in the world.

- **Hire a coach.** If you are ready to get serious about creating success, you will most likely use a combination of mentoring methods. One that you should definitely consider is working with a coach. Interview several coaches before you actually hire one. Have a list of questions that pertain to your situation and ask them all the same questions. One thing to keep in mind is that you are not looking for someone who will just make you feel good. You want someone who will challenge you. If you want to be successful, much of the work is about expanding your comfort zone. See who you build a rapport with, and be careful that you do not overlook a coach who will hold you accountable and make you stretch. Ask them about their methods for holding a client accountable.

How to Find a Mentor

Whether you choose to hire a personal coach or seek out a mentor who will share their time, here are some steps you can take to ensure that you find the right mentor for you:

- **Write** out your purpose or reason for wanting to work with a mentor or hire a coach. What are you hoping to achieve? What do you think your obstacles are? Make a list of specific questions that you want answered.

- **Ask** people you trust who might know someone in the industry or area in which you need mentoring. For instance, if you are struggling with getting clients, look for someone who has been through that struggle and mastered it. If you are wanting to get your music out to the world, find someone who has the expertise to help you record and market your CD. You can also search out mentors and coaches online or in business directories. Make a list of three to five possible coaches and mentors before you contact any of them.

- **Contact** all of the mentors or coaches on your list and tell them what you are looking for. Ask everyone the same questions, and make notes during and after each interaction. This process will help you narrow the list down so that you can make your final choice.

How to Work with a Mentor

Finding the right mentor is the first part of the process. Now we will explore how to work with a mentor. Keep the following steps in mind to help you deepen the relationship:

- **Respect your mentors' skills and time.** Mentors have reached this status by the very nature of having become successful. They spent a lot of time and energy to build their skills and knowledge base. Although they have mastered the skill that they are sharing with you, most mentors are on a continued growth journey for themselves and are, therefore, doing their own work, mastering other skill sets. Be mindful of their time and respectful of who they are.

- **Anticipate what you wish to learn from your mentor.** Know what it is that you want to work on within yourself. Be clear on your reason for working with a mentor in the first place. Although the conversation or coaching session will naturally produce more questions as you go and your intention or vision may deepen, it is nevertheless very help-ful to begin with knowing what it is that you want.

- **Be accountable.** When working with a mentor, arrive on time and come to the appointment having completed any of the previous steps to which you agreed in a prior meeting. It is also important to stick with the allotted time for your appointments and avoid re-scheduling. Of course, things occasionally come up and you or your mentor may need to change plans. Still, work toward consistent, committed times. Being accountable is one of the fundamental habits of success. It will help you develop in ways you never imagined possible. Successful people are accountable to themselves and to the people with whom they are involved. Be accountable and you will have mastered one of the most valuable success skills.

Other Ways of Supporting Your Success

In addition to having a mentor or hiring a coach, there are a number of ways to support your growth and progress as a mom entrepreneur that require the assistance of others. The following ideas are inexpensive and often free, although each requires time, persistence, commitment and care.

- **Modeling.** Successful people watch and listen to other successful people and then use the same methods and processes that they use. In this wonderful world of online access, finding successful people to model yourself after is easily done. Many experts hold free teleseminars on a regular basis, and if you find one that truly resonates with you, you can choose to study further with that person through his or her courses, books, audiotapes or workshops. See what others are doing in the area you have chosen to develop for yourself; they hold a treasure trove of experience.

- **Mastermind groups.** There is a lot of information available online about how to create and run a mastermind group. Basically, a mastermind group consists of a group of people who want to support each other to create success. They will brainstorm ideas with each other, share resources, and hold each other accountable. Generally, members of these groups check in with each other once per week to discuss their accomplishments and failures over the previous week. There is a level of accountability within the group so that everyone stays on track for the goals that they have personally stated they want to achieve. If you are someone who can be accountable to yourself and work independently, this could be a good choice.

- **Buddy coach.** Similar to a mastermind group, this is done one-on-one. You find a buddy to connect with—perhaps another mom entrepreneur—and you support, encourage and hold each other accountable. You may choose to meet or talk every day for 20 minutes or you may choose to connect once a week. My buddy coach and I check in with each other once per day, unless there are circumstances that prevent us from doing so. Our focus is simply to help each other stay accountable for what needs to be done. We state our goals for the day and then, on the following day, discuss whether or not they were achieved. You and your buddy coach can create guidelines together to suit your needs and lifestyles.

Take Your Life to the Next Level

If you are ready to take your life to the next level in any area, using these methods will help you accomplish your goals and create the life you truly wish to live. You do not need to go it alone when there are so many people who can provide you with the insight, encouragement and processes you need to have more success in your life. I encourage you to find a mentor and/or a coach and begin taking the high road to success.

Schall Adams

Personal Development Entrepreneur
Create an Amazing Life!

(775) 412-1891
success@schalladams.com
www.schalladams.com

Schall is a wildly fun transformational speaker and author who shares her love of life by teaching people to grow using her proprietary "Create an Amazing Life" programs. With this process, she teaches you to find your soul's purpose, connect to your passions, express them, make a difference through them, and continue to grow and expand your personal capacity.

Schall speaks regularly around the country. Her main topics include *Expanding Personal and Professional Capacity*, *How to Achieve Optimal Health*, *The Importance of Mentorship* and *Women's Issues*.

Schall left the corporate world at age 47. In just four years she has co-authored two motivational books, signed with a publishing house for her own book, recorded a music CD with an amazing band, developed a training program for raw food teachers who want to build their own businesses and founded an organization to help women around the globe mentor each other.

Schall is a co-author in *The Power of the Platform—Speakers on Life*, which is a compilation and anthology of some of the world's leading motivators and personal development experts including Jack Canfield, Arielle Ford, Brian Tracy and Les Brown. You can follow Schall at www.facebook.com/schalladams and www.twitter.com/schalladams.

Intuition: The Way of the Mommy Warrior

Your Secret Weapon in Business and Life

By Maria Salomão-Schmidt, MBA

> *"It is always with excitement that*
> *I wake up in the morning wondering what my intuition*
> *will toss up to me, like gifts from the sea.*
> *I work with it and rely on it. It's my partner."*
> —Dr. Jonas Salk, American discoverer of polio vaccine

What a ride it is being a mom who owns her own business! It is a deep, magical journey of learning, loving, and letting go. To be successful at it takes a large quantity of resources and abilities. One of the biggest challenges is the number of "to do list" items that never seem to go away, no matter how hard you work at it. Even if you have an assistant, nanny, partner or staff, ultimately you are still the captain of the ship and most everything still goes through you. However, it is impossible to do everything. The question is: how do you choose what to do and what to let go of?

Often when you are in the thick of things, *everything* seems important and you end up sacrificing yourself, sometimes to the extreme, for your business and family. Over time, if you keep struggling instead of allowing your life to flow, you begin to move further and further away from who you are. The deep joy you had around your business and your motherhood dissipates. You feel more lost and confused and perhaps guilty, too. Take this as important feedback. It is a sign you have gone into what Abraham Maslow calls the lowest rung of your "hierarchy of needs." You are running on adrenaline. If you were a car, you would be running on fumes. You have gone into survival mode. It is very important to know that you cannot achieve a sustainable business and family life in this mode. Many mothers live in this painful place because they don't know how to get out of this cycle. Today, you will become one of the few who will know how to break this cycle.

"Follow your instincts.
That's where true wisdom manifests itself."
—Oprah Winfrey, American media icon,
actress and philanthropist

The Whole Human Package Deal

If you are indeed feeling overwhelmed by the demands and responsibilities of being a mom entrepreneur, you are not alone. Compared to even a generation ago, the amount of information and activities you are responsible for today has dramatically increased. To help you adjust to this faster flow of life, it is more important than ever to access your intuition.

If you have a body and you are breathing, then you have intuition. It comes with the package deal you got when you entered Planet Earth. What happens, however, as with most package deals, is that we do not take the time to explore all the amazing offerings that came with it.

Intuition: the ability to understand something immediately,
without the need for conscious reasoning.
—The Oxford Dictionary

Meet Your Intuition

Intuition, our sixth sense, is one of the most powerful tools we have at our disposal. Many people do not even know that they have intuition. They may have received intuitive "hits" throughout their life and did not recognize that it was their intuition. A simple and common example is when we think of someone and moments later that person calls. It is my experience that mothers are keenly aware of their intuition—constantly intuiting the needs of the moment. Because you are a mom entrepreneur, it is my guess that it was your intuitive voice that led you to start your own business.

Intuitive messages come to you in any number of ways: a "knowing" feeling, pictures, voice or symbols. At first, you may confuse the voice of fear with your intuition. However, the more you pay attention, the more you will see the difference. That is part of the learning.

I like to frame it like this: when you were born, a series of gifts came along with receiving a body as well as receiving breath. It was the package deal, just like with the package of getting your phone, internet and cable, all in one deal, except this is much more thrilling!

All human beings are made up of three elements: mind, body and soul. Let's explore these one by one.

> *"You must train your intuition. You must trust the small voice inside you which tells you exactly what to say, what to decide."*
> —Ingrid Bergman, Swedish-American actress

The Mind

In school as children, we learn that we have five senses: sight, smell, taste, hearing and touch. Those are the senses that are hooked up to our brain. This information is socially acceptable, because we are currently a brain-centric society. Yet there is so much more. For example, there is your sixth sense of intuition. Intuition, however, does not register in the brain because it is not associated with the brain. The mind is a vital part of you. It works 24 hours a day, non-stop. However, your mind can only give you a fraction of what is so for you. Have you ever seen a hose squirming all over the lawn, getting everything wet because it has too much water coming out of it? That is what your mind is like when it is in charge. If you are not conscious of your soul being present, the mind will take over by default and the result is a scattered, stressful life with no focus. Your brain best serves you when it is working under the guidance of your body and soul.

> *"The intuitive mind is a sacred gift and the rational mind is a faithful servant. We have created a society that honors the servant and has forgotten the gift."*
> —Albert Einstein, German-American physicist
> and Nobel Prize winner

The Body

Another important element in the human package is our body. In Western society, women especially tend to take their bodies for granted and actually put them down. Having a body directly connects you to the wisdom of the universe. Bring that awareness into your life and feel it.

Your body is amazing! Now what are you going to do with it? How will you use it on this planet? Will you continue to work like a dog, always trying to cram in more, living in the lands of "keeping busy" and "should" and then burn out? Or will you take care of it, treasure it and enjoy it? It's your life. There is no right or wrong answer. There is only choice and the choice is yours.

Your amazing body is one of *the* most magnificent creations on this planet. It is a temporary temple for your mind and soul. The body gives you the power to create, which is an important part of intuition. The body also loves movement. Mom entrepreneurs sometimes eliminate exercise from their lives because they are so busy. In reality, the more inactive your body is, the less intuition you will have, because part of your tuning mechanism, your body, is not fully present in the equation of your life. The more you move your body, the more your intuition will develop.

"Have the courage to follow your heart and intuition.
They somehow already know what you truly want to become.
Everything else is secondary."
—Steve Jobs, American business magnate and inventor

The Soul
The soul is where your authentic self and your passion live. The soul is that part of you that society is only now beginning to publicly accept and explore. It is your life force. It never dies. It is the same energy that creates seasons, mountains, oceans, stars and even watermelons. Your mind and body die, yet your soul is eternal.

The Power of Now
Mom entrepreneurs, especially, always look for ways to do things better and faster so they can eventually get to that magical place of being *done*. In that magic place, you think you will have a good workflow going, you will make more money, your kids will be happy and then you can finally catch up on your sleep. You are striving for a place that only exists in your mind. However, that does not prevent you from trying to attain it. You run the risk of burn-out, running this endless race where the finish line never comes.

Much of the advice out there tells you to take care of yourself first. What does that mean? We are told to take bubble baths, meditate, make lists, follow lists and get massages. However, if you are not living your life in the present, savoring what is going on around you, all these suggestions just turn into more to-do list items and ultimately just stress you out even more.

Through my workshops, I have found that people spend about 30 percent of their lives thinking about the future, 50 percent thinking about the past and 20 percent thinking about the present. It is the same concept that you learn in business school. It is the 80-20 rule, which means that you spend 80 percent of your life thinking about the past or future, even though it is in the present moment that you hold your true power. The present moment is the only place you can directly access your soul. Those of us who are happiest and feel most fulfilled have lives in which the mind and body *serve* the soul. Noticing how you show up in the present and what you attract helps you move toward the life of your dreams.

> *"I feel there are two people inside me—me and my intuition.*
> *If I go against her, she'll screw me every time, and if I follow her,*
> *we get along quite nicely."*
> —Kim Basinger, American actress

Secrets to Growing Your Intuition

Like most human abilities, intuition needs to be developed. A common way that many are exposed to large doses of their intuition is when they are dealing with a tragedy, death or illness. When in these highly stressful situations, people's minds cannot handle what is going on and often shut down. All that is left is the presence of the soul in the current moment. People report that it is during these times that they really feel most alive because they are fully present in their lives. It is important to note, however, that you do not need to be in crisis to activate your intuition. There are other ways to get your brain to befriend your soul so that your life begins to unfold the way you dream about it in your mind.

Exercises to Build Your Intuition

Here are a few very effective ways to practice connecting with your soul. These are exercises you can teach your kids too. Many kids tend to zone out, spending large amounts of their time on video games, cell phones, movies, television, texting and computers. These activities keep them in their minds and away from connecting to their souls. Help bring them back to their souls using one or more of the following exercises, and try them yourself, of course!

Sleeping beauty exercise. Keep a journal by your bed. Before you go to sleep, ask a question to the universe, or whatever god you pray to. Think of one simple question—the simpler the better—then go to sleep. Remember, the brain is a machine that runs 24 hours a day. While you sleep, it is still working, and you can harness its power by allowing it to connect to your soul while you sleep. When you wake up in the morning, write what you remember from your dream in your journal. It may be a clear and obvious answer to your question or it may not seem to have anything to do with it at all. Give it time to settle in and reveal itself. An additional step you can take is to create another journal entry where you ask the dream what it came to teach you. Often, many amazing things are discovered by taking this step.

Yummy strawberry exercise. Grab the biggest, juiciest, organic strawberry you can find. Look at it. Smell it. Feel it. Your goal here is to take 15 minutes to eat it. The point is to be in the moment and just look at it for a while. Most likely you have eaten thousands of strawberries in your life. However, after doing this exercise, you will see things you never noticed before. At first, you might hear your mind saying how ridiculous this is and how you don't have time for this. That is good feedback for you because that is what is happening every time you try to connect with your soul. Do not judge, just bring awareness to it. Simply notice. Keep breathing and looking at the strawberry. Do not bite into it for at least five minutes. Bring awareness to how you feel.

Succulent silence. Silence is one of the most magical gifts we have on this planet and one of the most underrated. Ask your higher power for help and then sit in silence. Listen. In the moments of silence, your intuition will speak to you. You may want to write down what is revealed. The more you do it the better it will feel and the clearer information you will get.

Playing with Mama Earth. Mama Earth is also a mom entrepreneur. She runs and births the world just like you do. There are many lessons to learn from simply watching how things run in nature. You are part of the original "world wide web"—that of Mother Earth. There is nothing that happens that does not affect everything around it. Human beings are awakening to what we are doing to our planet. By bringing your kids of all ages—or even your staff—into the outdoors, you will automatically show them how to connect to their souls. Go on a simple nature walk, walk slowly, touch the trees, look up, look down, breathe in deeply. If you let yourself go, you will connect more deeply to your soul. When you connect to your soul, you open yourself up to more prosperity. How good does that feel? Your kids will feel better. Your employees will feel more loyal and happy. You will feel at peace.

Creating the Results You Want

Passion is a key ingredient to manifesting what you want your business and family life to look like. Whatever you focus on and add a charge to, you create in your life. Here is the manifestation formula:

Awareness + Strong Charge = More of That Result in Your Life

If you have bills (awareness) and then add deep feelings of not being able to pay for them (the charge), then you are sending out a demand for more bills and the inability to pay them. Gently begin noticing what is going on and change your attention to things you want to promote in your life rather than things that don't work.

There are so many wonderful gifts to help you live the life you want. To get there, it is going to take practicing skills that are inborn and that need to be developed. The biggest one is intuition. No matter how lost you may feel, you can connect to the wisdom that has always been and will always be there to gently guide you to the life of your dreams.

Maria Salomão-Schmidt, MBA

**Brick House Realty, Inc.
and ButterflyMoms**

(617) 877-3616
maria@butterflymoms.com
www.butterflymoms.com
www.brickhouserealty.com

Maria Salomão-Schmidt, mother of five and founder of Brick House Realty, has lived a rich and full life as a mom entrepreneur. It was one particular incident in her life, when her precious 13-month-old daughter Sophia "Butterfly" died in her arms, that Maria set a new direction for her life. It was her heartfelt search for meaning from Sophia's life and death, while still working, that birthed the concept of ButterflyMoms. Maria's work celebrates the spirituality of motherhood by helping women feed their authentic selves, their souls.

Before starting her entrepreneurial adventures, Maria worked in corporate America with Jack Canfield, MathWorks®, Jane Goodall, Citizen Schools, Yahoo!®, Mikhail Gorbachev, Reebok®, Glide®, Procter & Gamble®, Webgrrls®, Delta®, CBS®, Girl Scouts®, Sun Microsystems®, Internet World® and Xerox®.

Maria's ability to captivate and energize an audience has won her rave re-views. She is increasingly sought after as an expert resource on the subjects of business, entrepreneurship and motherhood. Maria has appeared in *Entrepreneur*, *Marie Claire* and *The Boston Globe* and on National Public Radio.

She has a master's in business from Simmons College and a bachelor's in communications from Boston College. She is currently enrolled in the Rhys Thomas Institute for Energy Medicine.

More MOM ENTREPRENEUR *Extraordinaire*

*N*ow that you have learned powerful tips on how to be a mom entrepreneur extraordinaire, the next step is to take action. Get started applying what you have learned in the pages of this book.

We want you to know that we are here to help you meet your professional and personal objectives.

Following is a list of where we are geographically located. Regardless of where our companies are located, many of us provide a variety of services over the phone or through webinars and we welcome the opportunity to travel to your location.

You can find out more about each of us by reading our bios at the end of our chapters or by visiting our websites listed on the next two pages.

When you are ready for one-on-one consulting or group training from any of the co-authors in this book—we are available! If you call us and let us know you have read our book, we will provide you with a free phone consultation to determine your needs and how to best serve you.

United States

California

Jennifer Bressie   www.jenniferbressie.com
Sheri Cockrell   www.womensbusinessplanning.com
Hope Desroches   www.sellitevents.com
Rhonda Johnson   www.igniteyourfinances.com
Cindy Sakai, MAOM, CDC   www.think-training.com
Tammy Tribble   www.mimeticdesign.com

Hawaii

Sarah Kalicki-Nakamura, MAOM, CDC   www.think-training.com
Grace Keohohou   www.dswa.org

Illinois

Martha Staley, CDC   www.directsellingsuccessstrategies.com

Louisiana

Karen Tucker, CDC   www.howtobepersistent.com

Massachusetts

Maria Salomão-Schmidt, MBA   www.butterflymoms.com

Nevada

Schall Adams   www.schalladams.com

Pennsylvania

Holly Chantal, M.Ed   www.websitegrowthcoach.com
Tara Kennedy-Kline, CDC, DCGL, MWP www.tarakennedykline.com

South Carolina

Teisha Shelby-Houston   www.thebusinesscoachformoms.com

Washington

Audrey L. Godwin, CPA   www.thegodwingroup.net
Leslie Irish Evans, LMP, NBCR, CA www.leslieirishevans.com
Molly Klipp   www.mollyklipp.com
Jennifer Malocha, AAS, ACSM, NSCA www.wuhoofitness.com

Canada

Alberta

Patti Snyders-Blok   www.rarepassions.com

Ontario

Tania Boutin, CLC, NLSC, SDC www.taniaboutin.com

THRIVE Publishing develops books for experts who want to share their knowledge with more and more people. We provide our co-authors with a proven system, professional guidance and support, producing quality, multi-author, how-to books that uplift and enhance the personal and professional lives of the people they serve.

We know that getting a book written and published is a huge undertaking. To make that process as easy as possible, we have an experienced team with the resources and know-how to put a quality, informative book in the hands of our co-authors quickly and affordably. Our co-authors are proud to be included in THRIVE Publishing books because these publications enhance their business missions, give them a professional outreach tool and enable them to communicate essential information to a wider audience.

You can find out more about our upcoming book projects at
www.thrivebooks.com

Also from
THRIVE Publishing™

Incredible
BUSINESS
Expert advice to accelerate your success

Vernice Armour
Victoria Ashford
Kathy Carrico
Karen Clark
Sheri Cockrell
Mike Coy
Sylvia Dolena
Pat Duran
Jennifer Howard
Dezi Koster
Mary Kot
Nancy LaMont
Joanne Lang
Tiffany Nielsen
Suzanne Zazulak Pedro
Marge Piccini
Caterina Rando
Suzie Read
Marsha Reeves Jews
Karen Sladick
Sylvia A. Stern
Darlene Willman

For more information on this book, visit
www.incrediblebusinessbook.com

Also from
THRIVE Publishing™

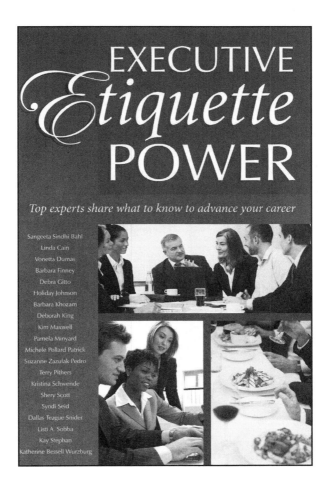

EXECUTIVE
Etiquette
POWER

Top experts share what to know to advance your career

Sangeeta Sindhi Bahl
Linda Cain
Vonetta Dumas
Barbara Finney
Debra Gitto
Holiday Johnson
Barbara Khozam
Deborah King
Kim Maxwell
Pamela Minyard
Michele Pollard Patrick
Suzanne Zazulak Pedro
Terry Pithers
Kristina Schwende
Shery Scott
Syndi Seid
Dallas Teague Snider
Listi A. Sobba
Kay Stephan
Katherine Bessell Wurzburg

For more information on this book, visit
www.execetiquette.com

Also from
THRIVE Publishing™

For more information on this book, visit
www.getorganizedtodaybook.com

Also from
THRIVE Publishing™

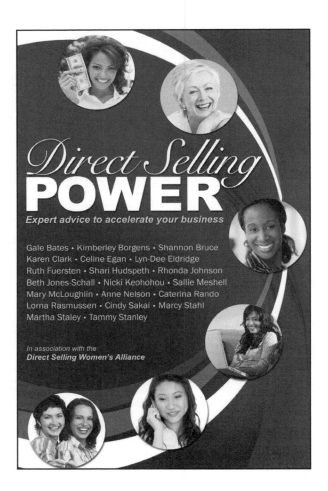

Direct Selling
POWER
Expert advice to accelerate your business

Gale Bates • Kimberley Borgens • Shannon Bruce
Karen Clark • Celine Egan • Lyn-Dee Eldridge
Ruth Fuersten • Shari Hudspeth • Rhonda Johnson
Beth Jones-Schall • Nicki Keohohou • Sallie Meshell
Mary McLoughlin • Anne Nelson • Caterina Rando
Lorna Rasmussen • Cindy Sakai • Marcy Stahl
Martha Staley • Tammy Stanley

In association with the
Direct Selling Women's Alliance

For more information on this book, visit
www.directsellingbook.com

For more information on any of these books visit:
www.thrivebooks.com

MOM
ENTREPRENEUR
Extraordinaire

Top experts share strategies for success

In collaboration with the Direct Selling Women's Alliance

Schall Adams • Tania Boutin • Jennifer Bressie • Holly Chantal • Sheri Cockrell
Hope Desroches • Leslie Irish Evans • Audrey Godwin • Rhonda Johnson
Sarah Kalicki-Nakamura • Tara Kennedy-Kline • Grace Keohohou • Molly Klipp
Jennifer Malocha • Cindy Sakai • Maria Salomão-Schmidt • Teisha Shelby-Houston
Patti Snyders-Blok • Martha Staley • Tammy Tribble • Karen Tucker

For more copies of *Mom Entrepreneur Extraordinaire*,
contact any of the co-authors or visit
www.momentrepreneurbook.com

About the Direct Selling Women's Alliance

The Direct Selling Women's Alliance began around a typical kitchen table when a group of women shared the vision of providing an opportunity for others to live their lives more fully while balancing their personal and professional needs. Never, in the 100+ year history of the direct selling profession had there been an association dedicated to the needs of independent network marketers and party plan professionals. Entrepreneurs from around the world now have a place to call their own: an alliance designed with their success in mind, an alliance to support the direct selling profession.

The DSWA provides a resource-rich website and cutting-edge virtual training courses specifically designed for direct sellers. We enrich the industry by providing personal and professional training through live and archived teleclasses, a learning library, collaborative leadership retreats, live events and much more. The DSWA also offers extensive benefits geared toward making life easier, such as options for health care, discounts on office supplies, free e-books and local chapter meetings.

We are excited to say that what began with a kitchen table discussion has grown into an international association boasting members from around the globe. The multiplying effect of touching women's lives has overflowed into direct selling companies, across gender and race, and into the next generation. One example of this phenomenal momentum is the *Build It BIG* and *More Build It BIG* books, which reached the top positions on multiple bestseller lists and featured outstanding leaders.

Yet another result of the growth of DSWA is the DSWA Global Foundation (DSWAGlobalFoundation.org), which offers scholarships